DINNER IN THE *Beer* GARDEN

LUCY SAUNDERS

Publication date: 2013
Publisher: F&B Communications LLC
ISBN-10: 097698752X
ISBN-13: 978-0-9769875-2-9
Suggested categories: Beer, Cookbook, Pairing Beer and Food
Library of Congress Control Number: 2013951673
240 pages, more than 110 recipes, index
Cover design: Libby VanderPloeg
Front cover photography: Jennifer Marx
Author photo: Michael Wessel Photography
Food photos: Jennifer Marx, Roger Brown, Michael Wessel, Mark Roberts
Food stylists: Lee Egan, Nina Borrato, Gaylon Emerzian, Johanna Lowe
Prop stylists: Karen Johnson, Beth Shully, Lucy Saunders
Printer: Worzalla, Inc., Wisconsin
Printed in the United States of America

for my mother, Sally,

and my husband, Tom,

with love

ACKNOWLEDGMENTS

Thank you to Alaskan Brewing Co., Bell's Brewery, Inc., Founders Brewing Co., Full Sail Brewing Co., Goose Island Beer Co., New Glarus Brewing Co., Rogue Ales, Sierra Nevada Brewing Co. and Sprecher Brewing Co., Inc., for supporting the color food photography. Their investment helped cover costs of food styling, prop styling, and location photos. Thank you to all my backers on Kickstarter, for providing the final push for production. Thanks to Libby VanderPloeg for cover designs, layout, illustrations and extra help.

Food photos in the cookbook were shot on location in beer gardens, home gardens and parks. Thanks to Janet Balding and her family for hosting two months of photography, as well as Milwaukee County Department of Parks, Recreation and Culture. Thanks to Roger Brown and Gaylon Emerzian, Jennifer Marx and Karen Johnson, Michael Wessel, and Catherine Etzkorn and Linda Hader at Centerpoint, Chicago.

Thank you for early support and inspiration: Marietta Abrams and Peter Brill, Wendy Adams, Michael Agnew, Ryan Arnold, Susan Solnick-Asp, Bo Belanger, Eric Barny, Larry Bell, Laura Bell, Larry Bennett, Lee Birkett, Janet Bischoff, Mike Brenner, Graham Broadhurst, Lew Bryson, Jay Brooks, Fred Bueltmann, Cindy Burchfield, Deb & Dan Carey, Jimmy Carbone, Margaret Casey, Michael Chaltry, Jennie Chen, Thomas Cizauskas, B. Jack Clobridge, Gareth Cure, Elly Cyr, Tom Dalldorf, Daniel Del Grande, Steve Ehlers, Gaylon Emerzian, Jamie Emmerson & Irene Firmat, Dave Engbers, Heather Porter Engwall, Alyssa Eppich, Patty Erd, Sandra Evans, Jennifer Faulk, John Freyer, Clay Gordon, Ken Grossman, John Hall, David Hayes, Sara Hill, Tim Harper, Betsy & Jim Henrichs, Julia Herz, Mike Higgins, Karen Hobbs, John Holl, Jeremy Horland, Michael Horne, Ian Hughes, Jim Javenkoski, Ron Jeffries, Ezra Johnson-Greenough, Brett Joyce, Jack Joyce, Jaime Jurado, Mike Kallenberger, Cliff Kaplan, N.M. Kelby, Jeremy King, Robyn Klinge, Tom Korder, Carrie Kortokrax, Lyn Kruger, Geoff & Marcy Larson, Adrienne Lee, Keith Lemcke, Ken Limas, Wendy Littlefield, Jackie Valent Lucca, Anne Maedke, Bill Manley, Aaron Mateychuck, Gerri and Joe McBride, Dave McLean, Pamela McManus, Evan Meffert, Marie Melsheimer, Bill Metzger, Risa Meynarez, Ben Mims, Lisa Morrison, Alec Mull, Christine Murphy, Randy Mosher, Henry Newnan, John & Linda Norton, Karl Ockert, Shaun O'Sullivan, Karen Page & Andrew Dornenburg, Todd Parker, Bruce Paton, Sean Paxton, Patty Peterson, Adrienne Pierluissi and Bruno Johnson, Nunzino Pizza, Luc de Raedemaeker, Susan Rankert, Linda Rastani, Gary Rejebian, Mark Roberts, Michael Roper and Louise Molnar, Dan Roubik, Ashley Routson, Don Russell, Tom Ryan, Brook Scheiber, Rick Seemueller, Mindy Segal, Carolyn Sevos, Ilse Shelton, Beth Shully, Pete Slosberg, Josh Smith, Anne & Randy Sprecher, Bonnie Steinman, Mike Stevens, Nancy Stohs, Tim Surprise, Jonathan Surratt, Fred Swanson, Steve Tager, Kate Theis, Tom Taylor, Libby VanderPloeg, Amy Waldman, Katie Wallace, Christina Ward, Alan Wax, Ken Weaver, Gregg Wiggins, Becky Wright, and Lupe Zepeda.

Thank you to all the contributors, reviewers and testers, including Alton Brown, Lori Barthelmy, Stephen Beaumont, Joshua M. Bernstein, Lindsay Bosslett, Mike Chaltry,

ACKNOWLEDGMENTS

Jennie Chen, Randy Clemens, Gwen Conley, Lauren Downey, Karen Duffin, David Fierabend, Lori Fredrich, Rick Hadsall, Rosa & John Haggerty, Steve Hamburg, Jen Harmon, Zach Heise, AJ Hurst, Micheal Iles, Robyn Klinge, Adrienne Lee, Dan Leff, Paula Lorenz, Annette May, Jodi Marti, Sheryl Marshall, Julie McDonald, Sue Moen, Julie Pandl, Andi Pellici, Pam Percy and Marty Hintz, Donna Piasecki, Susan Rankert, Joshua Smith, Jen Stubbs, Jennifer Sutherland, Tom Taylor, January Tiberius, James Waller, Tom West, Rebecca Wright, Sandra Wu and Nancy Zucker.

With appreciation to the hundreds of breweries, organizations and businesses who have helped with research including Craft Beer Cellar's Kate Baker and Suzanne Schalow, JoLinda Klopp and Lynn Winter of Triskele's, Karen Leahy, Adrienne Pierluissi and Bruno Johnson of the Sugar Maple and Palm Tavern, Northern Brewer, American Club and Kohler Festival of Beer, Sue Kinas and Peter Northard of the Brewhouse Inn and Suites, Omar Andrietsch of Rumpus Room and Bartolotta's, Sendik's, Visit Milwaukee, Stephanie Lecci and Mitch Teich of WUWM Milwaukee Public Radio, Joy Cardin and Larry Meiller of Wisconsin Public Radio, Kristin Korovec, Wisconsin Public Television, Wendy Littlefield and Don Feinberg of Vanberg & DeWulf, Charlottesville and Nelson County, VA, Independent Garden Center Show, Visit Philly/Philadelphia Tourism, Dianna Stampfler of Promote Michigan, CVB Ludington, MI, Melissa Dowling, The Boelter Company, Boelter SuperStore, Brewery Supply Inc., Rastal and Chrislan Ceramics, Libbey Glass, S. S. Steiner, Inc., Spiegelau USA, Louis Glunz Beer Inc., Brewers Association, Master Brewers Association of the Americas, Madison Homebrewers & Tasters Guild and Great Taste of the Midwest, North American Guild of Beer Writers, Siebel Institute, and state brewers guilds.

With love and gratitude to family and friends, especially Tom, Sally, Margery & Maia, Tony & Amy, Julia, Katerina, Brit & Annabelle, Ginna, Gretchen, Wes, Piper, Lily & Lisa, Kate & Mark, aunt Anne, Al & Gail, Sarah, Jeff, Ryan, Molly & Bob, uncle Bob, Dave & Lee Ann, Bob & Lee, Mike, Woody & Amanda, David, Kelley & Ben, Rob, Mary, Melissa & Justin, Anne & Vijay, David & Renee, Vikram, Fred & Wing, Alice & Lucas, Cece, John, Polly & Jim, Joe, Anne & Taylor, Caronline, Ellen, Cal & Gina, Joe & Gerri, Julie & Stu, Sona & Gary, Marian & Andrew, Anna & Paul, Peg & Pedro, Jonathan & Jamielynn, Gaylon & Roger, Elise, Sarah & Doug, Mar & Pete, Betsy & Jim, Hal, and the Balding, Carter, Geilfuss, Gates-Miller, Jahn, Pierce, Piper, Saunders, Shankar, Theis and Woodruff families.

Dinner in the Beer Garden

TABLE OF CONTENTS

CHAPTERS & PROFILES

PHOTO: JENNIFER MARX

CHAPTER 1
APPETIZERS

CAULIFLOWER & CAPER FRITTERS

PHOTO: MICHAEL WESSEL

CAULIFLOWER & CAPER FRITTERS

- 1 medium head cauliflower (about a pound)
- 6 ounces witbier, plus more if needed
- ¾ cup flour
- pinch sugar
- ½ teaspoon finely ground white pepper
- 2 tablespoons minced roasted red pepper
- 2 tablespoons minced shallots
- 1 tablespoon chopped capers
- 2 cups grapeseed oil
- Shredded cabbage or mesclun greens, for serving
- 2 tablespoons minced scallions
- ¼ teaspoon kosher salt

1 Wash and section the cauliflower into 12-16 florets (sized for two bites) including a small portion of stem with each floret. Set aside to dry on paper towel.

2 In a medium-sized mixing bowl, blend the witbier, flour, sugar, and white pepper. Blend with a fork just until not lumpy and quickly stir in roasted red pepper, shallots and capers. If batter seems very thick, add a bit more witbier.

3 Prepare a deep fryer according to the manufacturer's instructions, or place 2 cups grapeseed oil in a 1-gallon, deep Dutch oven over medium-high heat. Bring oil to 375°F. While oil heats, prepare a baking sheet lined with brown paper or paper towel.

4 Using a pair of tongs, hold a cauliflower floret by the stem piece and swirl in batter until coated. Gently drop into hot oil, and repeat until 3-4 florets are cooking in the hot oil. Do not crowd the fryer, and use a pair of long chopsticks or wooden skewer to turn pieces so they brown evenly. Remove florets when fully golden brown, and let the oil return to 375°F before frying the next batch of florets. Use a mesh strainer to remove any browned bits of batter in between batches. Repeat until all florets are cooked.

5 Place on a bed of shredded cabbage or greens, and sprinkle with scallions and salt. Serve warm.

Pairing: Pair with an Oktoberfest or dunkel lager to balance the cabbage flavor of the cauliflower and spicy browned batter.

MAKES 6 SERVINGS (TWO FLORETS PER SERVING)

BOCK BEER PRETZELS

Food expert Alton Brown makes pretzels, but without beer that adds caramel color and aroma. I tweaked his recipe to use bock lager for extra flavor—these are best served warm, with butter, cream cheese, or spicy mustard.

- 1 envelope (2½ teaspoons) active yeast
- Pinch white sugar
- 2 ounces warm water (between 105°F and 110°F)
- 2 bottles bock lager, room temperature, divided
- 1 ounce unsalted butter, melted and cooled to lukewarm
- 3 to 3 ½ cups all-purpose flour
- ½ teaspoon salt
- 1 tablespoon canola oil
- 2 cups water
- 1 tablespoon baking soda
- 1 egg, beaten
- Coarse sea salt, seasoned salt or smoked salt

1 Place yeast, sugar and warm water in a glass measuring cup. Stir gently until yeast is blended and not lumpy. Set in a warm place until yeast blooms, about 5-10 minutes.

2 Decant 8 ounces lukewarm (warmed to 90°F) bock lager into a large stand-mixer bowl and save remaining beer for later use. Add yeast mix to the lukewarm beer in the bowl. Add melted butter and stir. Add 3 cups flour and salt into beer mix, stirring until dough ball forms.

continued

Have fun with pretzel shapes—the Philly Beer Week Beer Garden at the Four Seasons Hotel featured pretzels baked with Sly Fox beer, formed into the initials of the brewery

BOCK BEER PRETZELS CONTINUED

3 Set up stand mixer with dough hook and knead dough. Stop after 2 minutes and scrape sides and bottom of mixing bowl, and knead another 8 minutes, or until dough is shiny and smooth. Or, place the dough on a lightly floured board, and knead for 10 minutes. If the dough seems very sticky, add more flour by the tablespoon.

4 Rub a teaspoon of oil on your clean hands and form a dough ball; rub dough with oil and turn to coat sides of the mixing bowl with oil, cover with a wrung-out damp cloth, and place in a warm spot. Let the dough rise for one hour. Preheat oven to 425°F.

5 When dough doubles in size, turn out onto a floured surface, and punch flat. Divide dough into 12 balls (about 1.5 oz. each). Roll ball of dough into a rope about 16 inches long. then shape into twists or pretzels. To make a traditional pretzel, curl rope into a U, then fold each end over base of U, and pinch dough in place. Line 2 baking sheets with parchment paper and place formed pretzels on lined pans, 6 per pan. Place the pans of pretzels uncovered in refrigerator to set, 15 minutes, while you prepare bock glaze. If you prefer, make simple dough rounds, twists, or letters.

6 In a large saucepan, boil the water, remaining bock lager and baking soda. Once boiling, turn heat to low. Using a slotted spatula or mesh wok strainer, dip each pretzel into the hot liquid for 20 seconds, supporting pretzel so it won't lose its shape. Drain pretzel, and place on the baking sheet. Repeat until all pretzels are glazed; let them rest for 10 minutes.

7 Make egg wash by mixing an egg in a small bowl, add a teaspoon water, and whisk until smooth and yellow. Use a pastry brush to daub the pretzels lightly with egg wash, and sprinkle with coarse sea salt or smoked salt, according to taste. Place pan on upper middle rack in oven and bake 17-20 minutes, or until pretzels are well browned and crunchy. Bake each pan alone so pretzel tops brown evenly.

MAKES 12 PRETZELS

ZUCCHINI CUPS WITH CORN SALAD

If you have a leftover ear of corn, this appetizer will put it to good use, with zucchini and chopped tomatoes, cooked with couscous and spices.

2 large zucchini (at least 10 inches long and 2 ½ inches diameter)
⅔ cup boiling water
⅔ cup fresh corn kernels (about 1 ear)
⅓ cup couscous
2 tablespoons minced onion
2 tablespoons minced red bell pepper
1 tablespoon tahini
Salt and freshly ground black pepper, to taste
½ teaspoon paprika
Fresh lemon wedges

Pairing: Enjoy a dunkel or dark lager with sweet malt character to accent the browned vegetable flavors of the baked zucchini.

1. Wash and trim zucchini. Cut into 6 or 7 thick rounds, at least 1½ inches thick. Use the tip of a grapefruit spoon or a melon ball cutter to scoop out zucchini pulp and seeds in centers, to a depth of one inch. Arrange hollowed-out zucchini rounds on a parchment-lined baking sheet. Freeze the pulp and seeds to use in savory soups or green smoothies.

2. Preheat oven to 400°F. In a quart saucepan, bring water to a simmer and add corn kernels. Cook 3 to 4 minutes, then stir in couscous, onion, bell pepper, tahini, salt and pepper. Cook 2 minutes, then cover and turn off heat. Let couscous steep until fluffy, about 20 minutes. Fluff the couscous and taste, add more seasoning if needed. Use a teaspoon to fill the zucchini rounds. Sprinkle with paprika.

3. Bake 15 minutes, or until zucchini is browned on edges and tender. Remove from oven and let cool to lukewarm before serving. Serve with fresh lemon wedges to squeeze juice over the rounds.

SERVES 6–8 (2 PIECES)

KALE TOASTS

Jimmy Carbone, chef/owner of Jimmy's No. 43 in New York, offers a sophisticated bar menu from a tiny basement kitchen. This recipe gets a hit of umami from boquerones, the white anchovies from Spain. You can leave out the anchovy and garlic, and make a vegan topping with chopped dried cherries or cranberries and minced sweet onion.

1 bunch (8 ounces) Lancinato or Tuscan kale, washed, stemmed, then shredded (yields about 3 cups)
Juice of one lemon
¼ cup olive oil
¼ teaspoon smoked salt
4 white anchovy fillets (optional)
2 teaspoons minced garlic, or to taste
Pinch cayenne pepper
1 teaspoon Dijon mustard
3 tablespoons toasted pine nuts, chopped

1 Prepare kale and toss with lemon juice and 1 tablespoon olive oil. Rub leaves until evenly coated. Sprinkle lightly with smoked salt. Set aside.

2 Combine anchovy and garlic, and sauté in 1 tablespoon olive oil in a large skillet over low heat until garlic is golden. Remove from heat and mash in pepper and mustard. Toss kale in skillet with warm anchovy-garlic mixture and garnish with prepared pine nuts.

3 Serve with crispy flatbreads or pumpernickel toast.

MAKES 4 SERVINGS

Tip: Use the freshest kale possible for this salad—if the stems are discolored dark, with fibrous ends that are splayed and dried out, the kale is old and better cooked in a stew or soup. You can also add grated hard cheese such as Parmesan or Asiago for savory, salty notes.

Pairing: Jimmy suggests a spelt saison, but I found a black IPA to be a malty match for the garlicky kale.

CARAMELIZED GARLIC & ARTICHOKE DIP WITH CASHEW CREAM

Remember the goopy artichoke dip made with mayonnaise? This vegan version uses cashew cream to bind, and makes a delicious topping for homemade kale chips or sliced kohlrabi.

1 cup raw cashews
4 to 6 ounces cold water
1 teaspoon salt
1 teaspoon minced garlic
1 can (14 to 15 ounces) artichoke hearts, drained
2 tablespoons minced parsley
¼ cup diced roasted red peppers
¼ teaspoon lemon zest
2 tablespoons pitted kalamata olives
olive oil, for greasing dish
1 teaspoon red pepper flakes
Raw vegetables for dipping

1 Preheat oven to 350°F. Place cashews in blender and pour cold water in to cover by one-half inch. Add salt and garlic. Cover blender and hold lid in place. Puree on high until smooth and creamy. Add more water if needed to reach a creamy consistency.

2 Chop artichoke hearts with parsley, peppers, lemon zest and olives, and transfer mixture to baking dish (1 quart capacity). Stir in cashew cream and sprinkle with red pepper flakes. Place on middle rack in oven and bake 20-30 minutes or until browned and bubbly. Serve with raw vegetables for dipping.

MAKES 4 TO 6 SERVINGS

Tip: This recipe is very flexible and can be doubled to serve more. You can also used boiled and peeled sunchokes or white beans or chickpeas instead of the artichoke hearts.

Pairing: A yeasty golden ale or strong Maibock will match the garlic flavors and mineral notes from the artichokes.

CHEDDAR-OLIVE PINWHEEL BISCUITS

- 2 cups all-purpose flour
- 1 tablespoon baking powder
- ¼ teaspoon salt
- ¼ teaspoon cayenne pepper
- ½ teaspoon paprika
- 1 tablespoon sugar
- 1 to 1¼ cups heavy cream
- 1 cup finely grated sharp Cheddar, divided
- 2 tablespoons melted salted butter, divided
- ¼ cup olive tapenade or minced, pitted black olives
- 1 tablespoon minced parsley

1 Preheat oven to 425°F. Sift the flour, baking powder, salt, cayenne, paprika and sugar into a large mixing bowl. Make a shallow crater in the flour and pour in 1 cup heavy cream and ⅔ cup cheese. Quickly stir into a dough (add more cream if needed to make dough elastic) and turn dough out onto a large piece of parchment paper (at least 20 inches long) lightly brushed with 2 teaspoons melted butter (or spritz with nonstick cooking spray).

2 Fold the parchment over the dough ball and press dough into a rectangle about 8x12 inches, about ½-inch thickness. Peel away the parchment.

3 Sprinkle olive tapenade or chopped olives, remaining cheese, and minced parsley evenly over the biscuit dough. Use the parchment paper to guide rolling the dough into a jelly-roll shape, pressing along the edges lightly to keep filling in place. Use a long piece of heavy thread or cheese wire to cut the biscuit log into 12 pinwheels, about ⅔-inch thick. Slide the thread underneath the log of dough, perpendicular. Bring the edges of the thread or cheese wire together, wrapping the thread in a loop around the roll, and pulling the thread loop closed to cut the rolled dough evenly and avoid compressing the pinwheel shape.

4 Line a baking sheet with parchment paper. Arrange pinwheel biscuits on baking sheet about 1-inch apart and bake 12-15 minutes or until golden brown. Brush with the melted butter, if desired, and serve immediately.

Pairing: An English mild ale accents the savory edge of the Cheddar and olive combination.

MAKES 12 PINWHEEL BISCUITS

FOUNDERS ALL DAY IPA WITH CUCUMBER-MELON SUMMER ROLLS

PHOTO: ROGER BROWN

CUCUMBER-MELON SUMMER ROLLS

When I first tasted the Founders All Day IPA, I caught a whiff of melon and mango among the hops, and it made me think of a refreshing combination of ripe cantaloupe, cucumber, basil and chilis.

- 1 large avocado
- 1 teaspoon toasted sesame chili oil
- ⅛ teaspoon or more cayenne pepper
- 1 medium cucumber, about 8 inches
- 2 teaspoons salt, divided
- ⅓ to one half ripe cantaloupe melon (medium sized)
- 1 tablespoon minced fresh Thai basil
- 6 -8 rice wrappers (8.5 inch diameter)
- 1 cup finely shredded mild butter lettuce, green or red leaf lettuce

ALMOND DIPPING SAUCE

- ½ cup coconut milk
- ½ cup almond butter
- 2 tablespoons fresh lime juice
- 2 tablespoons Sriracha sauce (or to taste)

SERVES 6 TO 8

1 Peel, remove pit and slice avocado into thin strips; brush with toasted sesame chili oil and sprinkle lightly with cayenne pepper to taste. Peel, remove seeds, and julienne cucumber into narrow strips. Sprinkle with salt; place in mesh sieve over bowl to drain.

2 Peel, remove seeds, and julienne cantaloupe melon into narrow strips. Sprinkle with one teaspoon salt and place on a paper towel to drain. (You can prep melon and cucumber up to 24 hours in advance.)

3 Press cucumber to drain and place in mixing bowl with chopped Thai basil; toss to coat. Press melon to drain and add to the cucumber.

4 Fill a large bowl with warm water. Dip one wrapper in water for 4 seconds to soften. Lay wrapper flat. In a row across the center, place 2 avocado strips, cover with 1-2 tablespoons each of the julienned and herbed cucumber and melon, and sprinkle with a few shreds of lettuce, leaving about 2 inches uncovered on each end. Fold uncovered sides in, over the filling, then tightly roll the wrapper. Repeat with remaining ingredients.

5 In a small bowl, mix the coconut milk, almond butter, lime juice, and Sriracha. Warm in a sauceplan to blend if almond butter is too stiff. Serve rolls with almond dipping sauce.

continued

CUCUMBER-MELON SUMMER ROLLS CONTINUED

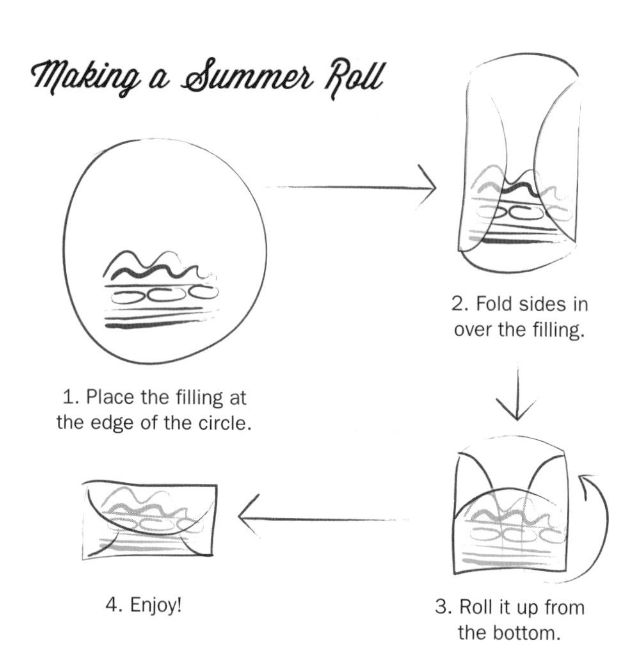

Pairing: Founders' hoppy All Day IPA melds wonderfully with flavors of Thai basil and melon; these spring rolls make beautiful little gem-like packages on the plate.

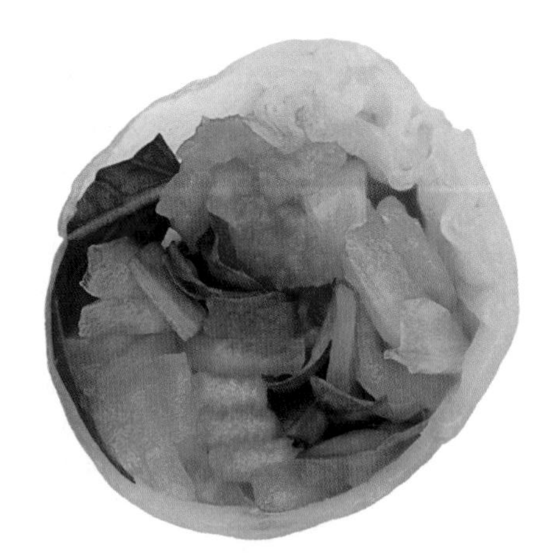

PUMPKIN EMPANADAS

A perfect recipe for a rainy afternoon or snow day, when you have several hours to make the dough and assemble these tasty two-bite empanadas! You'll need a food processor or grinder to make the sugar-pumpkin seed blend that makes these pumpkin empanadas so flavorful. Instead of the typical lard or shortening crust, this recipe features a yeasty masa dough which is lower in fat. Don't have time to make the dough? You can use frozen pie crusts, or 2 sheets of puff pastry.

1 To make the dough, measure ¼ cup water into a small bowl, sprinkle yeast over water, add sugar and stir gently. Set aside in a warm place to proof. Measure and place 2 cups flour and masa/corn flour in a large bowl; whisk to mix. Make a crater in the middle and add remaining lukewarm water, salt and 1 tablespoon oil. Add the proofed yeast and mix with your clean hands until dough forms a ball. If the dough seems dense or crumbly, add 2 to 3 tablespoons water to make an elastic dough.

2 Oil your hands so dough won't stick to your fingers. Knead dough 8 minutes, folding and turning, and adding more oil to your hands so dough becomes pliable, with small bubbles stretching on the surface as dough is kneaded. Coat the dough ball with about a tablespoon of the remaining oil, and place in an oiled bowl. Cover with a damp tea towel and place in a warm spot away from drafts, to rise until doubled, about 1-2 hours.

3 When dough has doubled, clean and oil your hands. Punch down the dough and flatten it. Divide dough into 24 balls. Place 1 inch apart on a floured baking sheet, and cover with plastic wrap. Let dough rest while you prepare filling.

continued

PASTRY

1¼ cups lukewarm water (105°F to 110°F)

2½ teaspoons (one envelope) active dry yeast

Pinch sugar

2¼ cups all-purpose flour, divided

1 cup masa or finely ground corn flour

1 teaspoon salt

3 tablespoons olive oil or pumpkin seed oil, divided, plus extra as needed

continued

PUMPKIN EMPANADAS CONTINUED

FILLING

- ½ cup lightly packed brown sugar
- 1 cinnamon stick, 2 inches
- ⅓ cup salted roasted pumpkin seeds
- 2 eggs
- 15 oz. pumpkin puree (do not use canned pumpkin pie mix)
- ½ cup minced sweet onion
- 1 tablespoon masa
- 1 tablespoon cream

Pairing: Perfect with a pumpkin ale or holiday spice ale to echo the warmth of the cinnamon and squash filling.

4 Place sugar, cinnamon stick, and pumpkin seeds in a food processor or blender fitted with the sharp cutting blade. Process on HIGH until cinnamon stick is ground and seeds are crushed. Add two eggs and process until smooth. Scrape the egg-sugar mixture into a bowl, and add pumpkin, chopped onion and masa. Mix well and set aside.

5 Assemble empanadas: mix the remaining egg with cream in a small bowl, whisking until smooth; set aside. Use a rolling pin to roll out each ball into a 4-inch diameter, on a clean wooden pastry board or masa-floured surface. Place a tablespoon of filling mixture on lower half of dough round. Dip your finger into egg cream, and moisten the edge of the top half of the dough round. Fold pastry over filling into a half-moon shape, and pinch edges together, crimping with the tines of a fork. Preheat oven to 375°F. Repeat until all the dough balls are filled and formed to make empanadas.

6 Place empanadas on a parchment-lined baking sheets about 1 inch apart. Brush lightly with oil and remaining egg-cream mixture. Bake 20-30 minutes or until well browned.

MAKES 24 EMPANADAS

THREE CROSTINI

Start with slices of bread, toasted or grilled with a swath of rustic toppings including olive oil, garlic, tomatoes and herbs and sometimes more elaborate mixes of olives, capers, tapenades, cooked beans and grilled vegetables. You can change the measurements according to the number of guests, as it's fun to assemble toppings according to taste. Simply make the prepared ingredients available to your guests, set out in bowls with spoons or tongs, and slide the custom-topped breads onto the grill for warming.

2 baguettes or ciabatta loaves, sliced ½-inch thick

INDIAN:

4 ounces paneer cheese, cubed very small
1 cup chopped roasted chiles
1 tablespoon minced ginger mixed with ¼ cup melted butter
1 cup cooked warm chickpeas, coarsely chopped, mixed with ¼ teaspoon ground cumin and ¼ teaspoon brown mustard seeds
1 cup steamed and chopped spinach

continued

MEDITERRANEAN:

6 ounces (wt) sliced tomatoes, seeds removed
3 tablespoons fresh chopped basil
3 tablespoons pitted oil cured olives
½ cup crumbled feta cheese
2 tablespoons capers
1 tablespoon olive oil

FRENCH

6 ounces (wt) brie, cut into small pieces
1 cup sliced and sauteed leeks
3 tablespoons chopped parsley
1 cup chopped golden tomatoes
¼ cup chopped walnuts

PHOTO: JENNIFER MARX

THREE CROSTINI CONTINUED

1 Start with about a cup each of the main ingredients, and a few tablespoons each of the condiments, spices, herbs, oils in squeeze bottles, and small dishes of chopped nuts. Each baguette round can only hold a tablespoon of the mixed topping, so plan on 3 slices bread per person.

2 Prepare each group of toppings as directed. From here, you can either mix the toppings in a single large bowl, or group small bowls of all the prepared ingredients on a tray. Supply your guests with toasted bread slices, and additional bowls if guests will be combining toppings as they like. Preheat grill or oven, and re-heat the toast slices with toppings to order, using a bread baking stone or baking sheet to keep the toppings intact.

Pairing:
Farmhouse ales with a yeasty bite will meld with the bread and herbal, salty toppings; try setting out several bottles of different saisons with small tasting glasses.

MAKES 6-8 SERVINGS, DEPENDING ON SIZE OF TOASTS

ABOUT TASTING AND PAIRING BEER WITH VEGETABLES

On a warm summer evening, I love to watch light filter through the leaves of the dogwood and viburnum, with a beer in hand, salad on the table, listening to the conversation of friends as I refill their glasses. "Why is it," I wonder, "that food and beer taste so much better together when we're in the beer garden?"

Perceptions are guided by experience (the garden, the company) and sensation (aroma, color, taste). And there's a delightful interplay between all those perceptions that I find fascinating. So, excuse me while I go a little geeky and explore some of the science behind flavors and beer pairing.

Hints for which type of beer pairs best with your favorite fruit or vegetable can be found in the food's essential makeup: from amino acids to minerals, plant compounds harmonize with beer flavors. And cooking unlocks these flavors.

Why focus on fruits and vegetables with paired with beer? Because I love the flavors and variety in produce—and beer. And I'm not alone. Joshua Bernstein, author of THE BEER COURSE (Sterling Epicure, 2013), says, "For me, nothing beats a Berliner weisse partnered with a freshly plucked salad dressed in vinaigrette."

The crisp mineral flavors in vegetables interplay with the taste of beer. Their mineral taste can be attributed to their higher concentrations of calcium, potassium and magnesium. You'll find mineral flavors in many leafy green vegetables and herbs—dandelion leaves, arugula, spinach, nettles, kale. The distinctive mineral aftertaste may make you yearn for a sweet, malty beer pairing—or a calcium-crisp IPA.

More flavors are unlocked through cooking fruits and vegetables. My food science guru, The Quantum Chef, explains. "Plants have minerals and glutamic acids, but require some kind of cooking process to convert to glutamates which carry savory, umami flavors," says Sebastian Buerba, editor of MolecularRecipes.com.

It turns out that fermentation is a prized cooking method for freeing flavor. Buerba reminds me that all cooking techniques—from brining and drying to roasting and smoking—will contribute in some way to the cellular changes that create flavor. But fermentation is the most reliable way of releasing the luscious and coveted umami flavors.

Think about your tastebuds, and what you perceive: the five elements of taste—salty, sweet, bitter, sour and savory umami—are foremost. Pour a glass of beer and ponder its possible pairings.

According to the late scientist, Morten Meilgaard, who wrote the textbook on sensory evaluation technique, "Flavor is the term used to describe the complex interactions of taste, smell, and chemical irritation of foods in the mouth that add to its mouth-feel, such as carbonation, the burn of chili peppers, or the coolness of menthol."

Taste can be classified into the five flavors listed above, but how many odors can we smell? According to a new study published in September 2013*, there are at least 10 broad categories of fragrance: fragrant/flowery, woody/resinous, fruity (non-citrus), chemical, minty/peppermint, sweet, popcorn, citrus/lemon, pungent and decayed. The list is a starting point to understanding the smells we perceive and how those perceptions relate to physical response.

With these fragrance categories in mind, turn back to your glass of beer. Inhale the aroma. What do you perceive? Do you detect flowery notes of Hallertau? Is it a wood-aged brettanomyces beer with aromas of old leather or oak barrels? Honing your fragrance perception will not only enhance your enjoyment of the beer, but guide you to more layered, subtle, and surprisingly rewarding pairings.

* PLOS ONE by Jason Castro from Bates College, Chakra Chennubhotla from the University of Pittsburgh, and Arvind Ramanathan from Oak Ridge National Laboratory

The subtly satisfying bitter, astringent or acrid sensations that certain vegetables create on the palate can be linked to compounds such as phenols and polyphenols, flavonoids, isoflavones, terpenes, and flucosinolates. Be warned that they may also have strong interactions in the body. One example: the purines found in spinach and mushroom can aggravate gout.

While I personally enjoy knowing some of the science behind flavor pairings, the most important pairing is the one that's in front of you. DINNER IN THE BEER GARDEN is written to enhance your dining at home, featuring recipes with fruits and vegetables at the center of the plate, paired with beer. You don't need the science to pay attention to taste. So, begin with your own preferences, guided by your senses.

Start with a sniff, not a sip. In tasting beer, aromas often suggest herbs, spices or other ingredients that might make a bridge for a food pairing. Your nose is a reliable and informative guide, conjuring sense memories of foods you've enjoyed.

The piney and resinous aromatics of hops may suggest rosemary or juniper berries. Citrusy hops meld well with tropical flavors such as mango or papaya, as well as tart berries such as cranberry, rose hips and goji berries.

Witbiers brewed with coriander and orange zest bring out the best in seafood and many salads. Malty, bready notes suggest caramelized flavors and meld well with rind-washed cheeses, dairy ingredients and eggs.

Peppery, high ABV brews will extend the heat of chiles and spicy foods. Yeasty dark ales balance the acidity in dark chocolate. Warming spices —cinnamon, nutmeg, clove, mace, ginger, white pepper, cardamom— can also balance high ABV and unfiltered yeast esters.

The appearance or texture of food can also give you key information. Before you start cooking with a piece of produce, look at it and taste it raw—is it dry or juicy? Color— bright or pale? Does the sliver have a detectable aroma? What is the taste—fresh and vibrant or dulled by shipping and storage?

In America, much of our produce is gassed and stored before shipping so aroma, flavor and nutrients dwindle. If you have vegetables that taste bland, turn to cooking techniques such as grilling, smoking, marinades and pan-roasting that can amplify flavor. And whenever possible, grow your own fruits and vegetables or buy them at local farm markets.

Leafy greens benefit from a bath in cold water to revive them. I often store herbs and greens such as fresh kale or chard, upright, with cut stems in a jar of water with a few drops of lemon juice added, to keep the leaves fresh until cooking.

Most of all, treat your fruits and vegetables with gentle respect in the kitchen—don't over cook them, or you'll lose aroma, texture and flavor.

Perceptions of flavor are influenced by experience and memory. In 1994, I interviewed Chef Jonathan Zearfoss, a professor at the Culinary Institute of America, about pairing tips. "The standard approach to flavors is to complement, contrast, or create a third new flavor through the synergy of flavor," he says.

"The taste memory is composed of the synergy between the drink and the food," says Zearfoss, "and that's especially true with beer since it has a definite aftertaste." Texture elements in beer—carbonation, residual yeast—also contribute to flavor.

Not long ago, I attended a tasting at the Craft Brewing Conference presided by Gwen Conley, director of quality assurance and the "Sensory Goddess" at Port Brewing/The Lost Abbey, and Julia Herz, craft beer program director at the Brewers Association. The two women rocked through a beer and food pairing session.

We reviewed how appearance, aroma, mouth-feel, and other factors such as emotional triggers can affect how we perceive taste. Gwen stressed that we will all perceive things differently and, that really, there are no right or wrong answers to the question, "What do you taste?"

Ultimately, there's no one formula to fit everyone's tastes. Use the pairings suggested in the recipes as a starting point—then experiment with your own matches. What you can count on is the delightful glow that comes from enjoying beer and food together, while basking in the beauty of the beer garden.

Cheers, Lucy Saunders

Dinner in the Beer Garden

CHAPTER 2

BEANS & LEGUMES

APPLE-BLACK LENTIL SALAD

PHOTO: MICHAEL WESS

APPLE-BLACK LENTIL SALAD

Lentils are so good for you, but typically so drab on the plate. This salad brings together small tender black lentils, with bright flavors of apple and red onion, tossed in tarragon and mustard dressing. You can substitute brown or green lentils, too, if black lentils are hard to find.

- **1 cup dried black lentils (2 cups cooked)**
- **⅔ cup diced green apple, tossed with ½ teaspoon lemon juice**
- **½ cup diced celery**
- **1 orange, peeled and segmented**
- **1 cup tomato wedges**
- **Oak leaf or butter lettuce (4 to 6 ounces)**
- **¼ cup tarragon vinegar**
- **1 teaspoon Dijon mustard**
- **¼ cup olive oil**
- **¼ teaspoon salt**
- **⅛ teaspoon cayenne pepper**

Pairing: Pair with hard cider or pale ale, to meld with the apple flavor and heighten the earthy taste of the lentils and mustard.

1 To prepare lentils, rinse in a colander and pick over to remove any grit. Place in 2-quart saucepan. Cover with water to 1-inch above the lentils, and bring to a simmer. Cook 15 minutes, or until lentils are just tender. Black lentils are smaller and cook faster than brown lentils. Let cool to lukewarm, then drain and add to mixing bowl.

2 While lentils cook, prepare apples, celery, orange and tomato wedges. Wash and trim the lettuce. Mix vinegar, mustard, olive oil, salt and cayenne in a small bowl, and whisk together to make an emulsion.

3 Toss the cool lentils with apples, celery, orange and tomato wedges, and dressing. Arrange four salad plates with lettuce leaves on edges. Divide lentil salad mixture evenly between the plates.

MAKES 4 SERVINGS

FULL SAIL AMBER ALE AND WHITE BEAN & ESCAROLE STEW

PHOTO: JENNIFER MA

WHITE BEAN & ESCAROLE STEW

Full Sail Brewing Co. offers vegetarian options with virtually every beer dinner the brewery offers. This stew tastes hearty and just a bit spicy, thanks to green chilies and adobo sauce in the broth.

- 1 pound dried white navy beans
- ⅓ cup olive oil, divided
- 1 cup corn kernels (fresh or frozen)
- 1 cup chopped celery, chopped
- ⅔ cup yellow onion, peeled and chopped
- 2 tablespoons minced garlic
- 1 chopped chile en adobo and 1 tablespoon adobo sauce
- 2 bay leaves
- 3 cups boiling water, plus more if needed
- 1 head escarole, cored, washed and chopped (about 3 cups)
- 1 15 oz. can diced fire-roasted tomatoes with green chiles, drained
- 1 teaspoon lime juice
- Salt
- Coarse ground black pepper

1 Pour beans into a colander; rinse in water and remove any debris. Place beans in a large bowl; cover with water to a depth of 2 inches above the height of the beans, and soak overnight.

2 Pour beans into colander and rinse. Place 1 tablespoon olive oil in a gallon stew pot over medium heat. Add corn, celery, onion, garlic, and minced chile en adobo. Cook vegetables in oil until soft, and add soaked beans and bay leaves. Stir to coat, and add boiling water to cover beans by ½ inch.

3 Reduce heat to low and simmer, covered, until beans are tender, about 2 hours. Stir occasionally and add more water if needed.

continued

Pairing: Full Sail Amber Ale makes a sweet partner to this dish, with its balanced malt character and spicy, aromatic hop finish.

WHITE BEAN & ESCAROLE STEW CONTINUED

GARNISH

12 -18 large fresh sage leaves
Toasted bread

MAKES 4 TO 6 SERVINGS

4 Remove bay leaves and stir in escarole, diced tomatoes, and lime juice. Cover and simmer 20 minutes,or until escarole is tender. Add a few tablespoons water if mixture seems too thick. Taste and season with salt and pepper as needed. Meanwhile, heat ¼ cup olive oil in large skillet over medium heat. Fry sage leaves until golden brown. Drain on paper towel and sprinkle with salt. Garnish stew with fried sage and serve with toasted bread basted with the sage oil.

PHOTO: JENNIFER MARX

CRISPY SESAME GREEN BEANS

Easy to make, and even easier to eat, according to one recipe tester, who estimated that she and her husband ate the equivalent of six appetizer servings by themselves. "They are that good, and the sesame sauce is wonderful as a dip," Annie says.

- **1 pound fresh green beans**
- **1 cup all-purpose flour**
- **12 ounces amber ale**
- **½ teaspoon freshly ground black pepper**
- **1 tablespoon white or black sesame seeds**
- **1 tablespoon minced garlic**
- **1 teaspoon salt**
- **2 -3 cups grapeseed oil**

Dipping sauce

- **¼ cup Sriracha**
- **¼ cup tahini**
- **¼ cup hoppy pale ale**
- **Juice of one-half lemon**

Pairing: Pair with a hoppy American pale ale, to match the lemon flavors in the dipping sauce and brighten the malty taste of the beer-battered beans.

1. Wash and pick over the fresh green beans, trimming off the fibrous stem ends. Don't remove the "strings" or the beans will split while cooking. Drain and dry the beans on a kitchen towel or tea towel. While beans drain, mix the dipping sauce ingredients in a small bowl, and set aside.

2. Whisk together the flour, amber ale, pepper, sesame seeds, garlic and salt in a 2-quart mixing bowl. Do not over mix or the batter will be tough. Set aside. Line a baking sheet with brown paper or parchment, and set aside.

3. Pour oil in a large deep Dutch oven or heavy cooking pot with high sides to a depth of two inches. Place over medium-high heat and bring to 350°F.

4. Dip 5-8 green beans in batter until coated; use long-handled tongs to place in the oil, do not overcrowd and do not let the beans stick together in the oil. Let the green beans cook until the batter is golden brown, about 3 minutes, and use tongs to lift the beans out of the hot oil, and move to the prepared baking sheet to drain. Use a mesh scoop to filter out bits of batter, and allow oil to re-heat in between batches. Repeat until all the beans have been cooked. Serve beans with the dipping sauce.

MAKES 4 TO 6 SERVINGS

CANNELINI BEANS, BEETS, CHARD

PHOTO: MICHAL WESSEL

CANNELINI BEANS, BEETS, CHARD & APPLE-MUSTARD DRESSING

This is a simple salad that can be extended with other ingredients, including diced green apples or toasted walnuts, if desired.

1 Mix white beans, beets, baby chard or arugula and scallions in a medium bowl.

2 Place 2 tablespoons olive oil in a nonstick skillet, and heat over medium-high. Tear off a small piece of sage leaf and drop in the hot oil. If it bubbles and sizzles, the skillet is ready to toast the remaining sage leaves. Lay the sage in the hot oil and cook on both sides. Drain on paper towel and sprinkle with sea salt and freshly ground black pepper, if desired.

3 Place apple, vinegar, celery seed, mustard and oil in a blender. Cover and puree on high until creamy. Taste and add salt and pepper, if desired. Garnish salad with dressing and crumbled cooked sage.

MAKES 4 SERVINGS

- **2 cups cooked cannellini or Great Northern white beans, drained**
- **1 cup sliced cooked red beets**
- **3 ounces baby chard or arugula, washed and drained**
- **⅓ cup sliced scallions**
- **2 tablespoons olive oil**
- **8 large sage leaves**
- **sea salt and freshly ground black pepper**
- **½ green apple, seeds removed and diced (about 1.5 ounces wt.)**
- **2 tablespoons balsamic vinegar**
- **¼ teaspoon celery seed**
- **1 tablespoon coarse mustard**
- **¼ cup olive oil or walnut oil**

Pairing: An apple ale melds with the flavors of the dressing and sage; the sweet fruity ale aromatics will match the mustard blend.

BLACK-EYED PEA FRITTERS WITH TOMATO-THYME AIOLI

PHOTO: MICHAEL WESSEL

BLACK-EYED PEA FRITTERS WITH TOMATO-THYME AIOLI

Tired of frites as the standard bar snack? These fritters are tender, bite-sized clusters of savory batter and peas.

- ⅔ cup all-purpose flour
- ½ teaspoon baking soda
- ½ teaspoon salt
- ½ teaspoon smoked paprika
- ⅛ teaspoon ground cayenne
- 1 can (14 oz.) black-eyed peas, drained, or 2 cups cooked black-eyed peas
- ½ cup minced scallions
- ¼ cup chopped flat leaf parsley
- 2 tablespoons chopped fresh thyme (or 1 teaspoon dried thyme), divided
- 2 eggs and 1 egg white, beaten
- 2 to 3 ounces spritzy Pilsner
- Vegetable oil or grapeseed oil for frying
- ½ cup mayonnaise or Vegenaise
- 2 tablespoons roasted garlic (see page 32)
- ½ teaspoon hot sauce, or to taste
- 1 cup fresh diced tomatoes, seeds removed

1 Whisk together flour, baking soda, salt, smoked paprika and cayenne in a medium mixing bowl, and set aside.

2 Drain black-eyed peas, and place in 2-quart mixing bowl. Add scallions, parsley, 1 tablespoon fresh thyme or ½ teaspoon dried thyme and toss. Stir in blended eggs and 2 ounces beer. Stir in flour mixture to make a batter. Set aside for 10 minutes.

3 Pour oil to a depth of 2 inches in a large, deep Dutch oven or heavy stockpot, and heat over medium-high until oil reaches 350°F. Line a baking sheet with parchment paper and heat oven to 275°F.

4 Stir the batter to distribute the ingredients; if it seems too thick, add more beer. Use a long-handled spoon to drop heaping tablespoons of the fritter mixture into the hot oil, but do not crowd the pan (about 5-6 fritters will fit into a 12-in. round Dutch oven). Use tongs to turn the fritters. They will be ready when golden brown, and when torn into, the batter is cooked through.

contiinued

BLACK-EYED PEA FRITTERS WITH TOMATO-THYME AIOLI CONTINUED

Pairing: Pair these fritters with an English brown or mild ale, to heighten the herbal flavor of the thyme and crispy crust to accent the malty ale.

5 Move cooked fritters to the prepared baking sheet and keep warm in the oven. Add more oil if needed and reheat to 350°F in between batches. You will have 20-24 fritters.

6 Mix mayonnaise, thyme, garlic puree and hot sauce in a small shallow dish. Sprinkle fritters with chopped tomatoes and remaining chopped fresh thyme. If using dried thyme, add to the dipping sauce.

SERVES 6 TO 8

Roasted Garlic:

3 heads garlic
1 teaspoon olive oil

Remove fibrous stem ends from each head of garlic, and remove any loose skin or debris. Remove one layer of garlic skin until outline of cloves is visible, but head is still intact. Rub garlic with oil and wrap in heavy foil. Bake at 350°F for 20-30 minutes, until garlic is soft and tender. Remove from oven and cool 15-20 minutes. When cool enough to handle, unwrap and slide the garlic cloves out of their papery skins by pressing from the stem end. Mash the cooked garlic with a bit of salt, and place in a resealable container. The roasted garlic paste may be frozen in teaspoon measures in a covered ice cube tray, and then transferred to a resealable plastic bag. Makes ½ cup.

CHANA MASALA WITH FIG-HONEY CHUTNEY

Indian food, especially curries, make a seamless match with IPAs; here, the fig-honey chutney provides a sweet transition to the hoppy ale.

- 1 cup diced onion
- 1 teaspoon minced garlic
- 2 teaspoons grated ginger
- 1 tablespoon minced fresh jalapeño
- 2 tablespoons vegetable oil
- ½ teaspoon brown mustard seeds
- 1 teaspoon turmeric
- 1 teaspoon cinnamon
- 2 cups diced ripe tomatoes in season (or 28 oz. can diced tomatoes)
- ¼ teaspoon ground cardamom
- 1 15 oz. can chickpeas
- Cooked basmati rice
- 2 tablespoons minced fresh cilantro leaves

CHUTNEY

- ½ cup chopped sweet onion
- 1 tablespoon coconut oil
- 8 ounces (fl) honey ale
- 4 ounces (wt) chopped dried figs (mission or calmyrna)
- ¼ cup honey such as buckwheat or raw ginger honey
- ½ teaspoon cinnamon
- 2 tablespoons chopped candied ginger
- 1 teaspoon tamarind paste or 1 tablespoon fresh lime juice
- Salt and cayenne pepper, to taste

1 Sauté onion, garlic, ginger, and jalapeño in oil in a large heavy skillet over medium heat; cook and stir until onion is soft. Add mustard seeds, turmeric, cinnamon and diced tomatoes (if using canned tomatoes, include juice).

2 Reduce heat to low, and add cardamom and chickpeas. Simmer 15 minutes over low heat. While masala cooks, prepare the basmati rice according to package instructions, and the fig-honey chutney, below. Serve the rice and chana masala garnished with minced fresh cilantro leaves, and pass the fig-honey chutney at the table.

3 Sauté onion in coconut oil in large heavy saucepan over medium heat. Add honey ale and figs. Simmer uncovered 5 minutes. Stir in honey, ginger, tamarind or lime, and cinnamon. Reduce heat to medium-low and cook until mixture is thick and figs are tender. Stir often. Taste and add salt and cayenne pepper if desired.

MAKES 4 SERVINGS

Pairing: Pair with an English bitter or IPA, to heighten the impact of the curry spices.

Bavaria's Biergartens

BY LINDSAY BOSSLETT & RICK HADSALL

On a perfect day—blue skies, 70°F, a light breeze whispering through the chestnut trees—while you're sitting at a long wooden table with a dozen strangers who are speaking, it seems, at least four different languages, you realize you're in a good place. And what makes the beer garden so beautiful, beyond the beer steins the size of your head?

During our first trip to Bavaria, we had several goals, but top of the list: "Visit beer gardens!" There are a few beer gardens near us in northern New Jersey and New York City. And perhaps it was our visits to these, or perhaps it's the beer gardens we've seen fictionalized that gave us the impression that "beer garden" was another term for "young people getting very drunk at an outside bar." We couldn't have been more wrong.

Oh, the German beer gardens do have lots of young people at them—not to mention a fair share of beer—but what surprised us most were the families. Older couples meeting up for a night out, parents with their kids in tow, grandma, grandpa and the neighbors from down the street. As we made our way from the more touristy gardens in the center of Munich (including, of course, the infamous Hofbräuhaus) to the suburbs, this became more and more true. To the Germans, beer gardens seem to be a way of life—a part of the community where everyone gathers to discuss politics and the weather over liters of dunkel and some crispy fried potatoes. And while there was the occasional rowdy table or two, for the most part everyone was content to relax and enjoy the food, beer, conversation and setting. There is a respect for the shared space and all who are experiencing it, be they tourists or locals.

To highlight the family-friendly atmosphere of the gardens, one of our favorites of the trip, Hirschgarten—which also happens to be the largest—even had stands selling ice cream and candy. Locals can watch their kids on the playground, grab some dinner and catch up on neighborhood gossip, all in one place. You could get a similar experience at the Chinesischer Turm (Chinese Tower) beer garden in the Englischer Garten—an expansive park right in Munich.

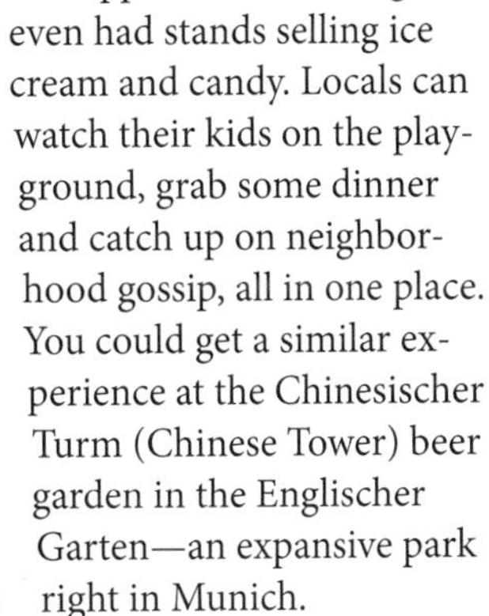

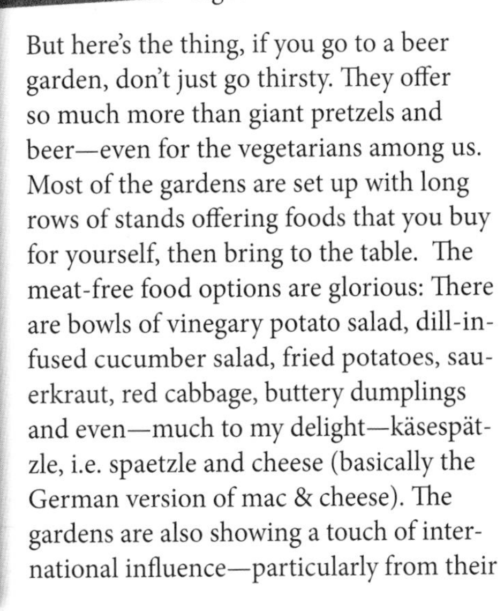

But here's the thing, if you go to a beer garden, don't just go thirsty. They offer so much more than giant pretzels and beer—even for the vegetarians among us. Most of the gardens are set up with long rows of stands offering foods that you buy for yourself, then bring to the table. The meat-free food options are glorious: There are bowls of vinegary potato salad, dill-infused cucumber salad, fried potatoes, sauerkraut, red cabbage, buttery dumplings and even—much to my delight—käsespätzle, i.e. spaetzle and cheese (basically the German version of mac & cheese). The gardens are also showing a touch of international influence—particularly from their

growing population of Mediterranean immigrants—with offerings like Greek salad.

On one of our last days in Munich, we sat down at a beer garden and began chatting up the people next to us at the table. It turns out that they were tourists, too, from a town not twenty miles from where we live in the States. We lingered long over beers and made heartfelt promises to keep in touch once we arrived back home—a promise we actually kept—as true friends made in a beer garden. And there's perhaps the greatest secret of all to these gems of Germany—they don't just support communities, but actually *build* them. ■

ABOUT THE CONTRIBUTORS

Lindsay Bosslett and Rick Hadsall are frequent travelers and enjoy food, drink and beautiful spaces around the world. Lindsay is a magazine editor and, as owner of Lindzer Studios, a freelance writer and photographer. Rick is a software development executive, part-time brewer, and a full-time beer and whisky aficionado.

ALL PHOTOS COURTESY OF LINDSAY BOSSLETT

CHAPTER 3
CHEESE

PHOTO: MICHAEL WESSEL

FARMSTEAD CHEESE TURNOVERS

Make savory turnovers for appetizers or brunch, with puff pastry baked with a simple filling of grated farmstead cheese and dried cranberries. Choose an artisanal or aged cheese with lots of umami, such as a bandage-wrapped white Cheddar or mature Gouda.

- **¼ cup flour, for rolling**
- **2 sheets puff pastry, thawed (1 pound package)**
- **1 large egg**
- **1 tablespoon water**
- **4 ounces (wt) sliced farmstead cheese or aged Gouda**
- **½ cup dried sweetened cranberries**
- **1 tablespoon sugar**

1 Preheat oven to 400°F. Sprinkle flour on a clean work surface. Unfold 1 thawed puff pastry sheet over the floured area. Rub flour on a rolling pin, and gently roll the pastry sheet into a 12-inch square. Cut into four even squares. Repeat with the remaining pastry sheet.

2 Whisk together egg and water in a small bowl until smooth. Divide cheese evenly among the pastry squares, placing along one corner (diagonally) so that the pastry forms a triangle when folded. Divide and arrange cranberries evenly on top of cheese. Lightly brush the edges of the pastry squares with a bit of the egg blend. Fold the pastry squares diagonally to form triangles. Press the edges of the pastries with tines of a fork to seal, or crimp with your clean fingertips.

3 Brush the turnovers lightly with the egg mixture, and sprinkle each with sugar. Prick the pastry lightly with the tines of a fork. Place the turnovers on a parchment-lined baking sheet. Bake 20 minutes or until turnovers are golden brown.

MAKES 8 TURNOVERS

Pairing: Pair with a strong Belgian ale brewed with candi sugar, to pick up the caramel and buttery flavors of the puff pastry. Serve with Meyer lemon marmalade or beer jelly, page 195.

HOP-AGED CHEDDAR & TOMATO GRILLED CHEESE

PROPS: BETH SHULLY / PHOTO: MICHAEL WESSEL

HOP-AGED CHEDDAR & TOMATO GRILLED CHEESE

A great way to add aromatics to a standard Cheddar is to age it over hop pellets or fresh hops in a food-safe container in the fridge. It's an adaptation of a technique called affinage, or aging cheese using special conditions such as cave flora or rind washes. You may not have a cave to call your own, but you probably can get your hands on a few ounces of fresh or dried hops in cones or pellet form. Check out homebrew supply shops such as NorthernBrewer.com.

3 tablespoons butter, softened
4 slices whole-grain bread
4 to 6 ounces hop-aged Cheddar, shaved or thinly sliced
1 heirloom tomato, sliced thick (2 tomatoes, if small)
4 -5 fresh basil leaves, julienned
2 tablespoons brown seed or coarse ground mustard

1 Heat a heavy saucepan or griddle (cast iron is best) over medium heat. Butter the bread slices on one side.

2 Place two slices of bread, buttered side down on the hot pan or griddle. Arrange half the shaved Cheddar over the bread and top with tomato slices. Sprinkle with the julienned basil. Place the remaining Cheddar over the tomatoes. Spread mustard on unbuttered side of sliced bread. Top the tomatoes with bread slices, buttered side up. Tent with a piece of foil, and cook several more minutes.

3 Check that bread is golden brown and cheese is melting. Flip and continue to cook until other side is toasted, another 2-3 minutes. Serve with salad or pickled vegetables.

MAKES 2 SANDWICHES

continued

HOP-AGED CHEDDAR & TOMATO GRILLED CHEESE CONTINUED

Pairing: Try a black IPA or schwarzbier, as the toasty malt will support the flavors of the hopped Cheddar and acidity of the tomatoes.

Tip: Put the hops in the bottom of a glass or stainless steel container. Place the unwrapped Cheddar on a small square of parchment paper and place in the container (you don't want the Cheddar to sit directly on the hops). Seal the container completely and let the hops infuse the cheese overnight. Taste the Cheddar and see how well you like the hops. If you want a stronger hops flavor, slice the Cheddar into smaller pieces, which will pick up more of the aromatics. This makes a fantastic grilled cheese sandwich with heirloom tomato slices and a smidge of mustard.

PROPS: BETH SHULLY / PHOTO: MICHAEL WESSEL

HOT CHEDDAR DIP WITH IPA

Gooey hot cheese and hoppy IPA, melted together and accented with rosemary-smoked shallots and hot pepper sauce—this is an addictive appetizer or topping for baked or grilled vegetables.

- Nonstick cooking spray
- 3 sprigs rosemary
- 2 or 3 shallots, peeled and quartered (about 3 ounces by weight)
- 2 tablespoons butter
- ¼ cup all-purpose flour
- ¼ cup heavy cream
- ½ teaspoon powdered mustard
- 12 ounces IPA, room temperature
- 10 ounces aged Cheddar, grated
- 2 ounces Parmesan, grated
- Hot pepper sauce, to taste
- Worcestershire sauce, to taste
- Dippers, such as baby carrots, celery sticks, crackers and toasted bread

1 Tear a sheet of foil at least 7 inches wide. Spray lightly with nonstick cooking spray. Place rosemary on center of foil, and mound shallots on top. Crimp edges of foil together to make a packet. Preheat grill to medium heat (350°F), and cook foil packet for 8 minutes. Or, if a grill is not available, place a cast iron skillet over high heat under a strong ventilation fan. Place foil packet in skillet and cook over medium-high heat for 6-8 minutes. Remove from heat and set aside to cool.

2 Melt butter in a large heavy saucepan over medium heat. Whisk in flour to make a roux, and cook until golden brown and flour smells like popcorn. Reduce heat to low. Whisk in cream and powdered mustard. Slowly drizzle in IPA, whisking constantly. Cook and whisk until smooth, then slowly add Cheddar by the quarter cupful, whisking after each addition. Whisk in Parmesan cheese, and taste. Add several drops hot pepper sauce and Worcestershire sauce, to taste. Remove from heat.

3 Unwrap foil packet and remove the softened smoked shallots. Chop very fine, and stir into the Cheddar IPA dip. Chop one tablespoon of the cooked rosemary leaves, and sprinkle on top. Serve warm, with dippers.

MAKES 3 CUPS

Pairing: More IPA! The hops in an American IPA match the resinous flavors of rosemary and cut through the buttery melted Cheddar. Or, if serving over grilled vegetables or using as the base for a potato gratin, serve with an ESB ale, with a balanced malt/hop profile.

CHEESE POLENTA WITH SWEET ONION MARMALADE & STRAWBERRY SALSA

Polenta can be breakfast, lunch, dinner—or appetizer, depending on how it's seasoned and topped. This makes a really wonderful side dish or main course, with caramelized onions cooked into a savory marmalade, and fresh strawberry salsa.

3 cups water
½ teaspoon salt
1 cup polenta or coarse corn grits (I use Bob's Red Mill)
3 ounces (wt) Gouda (or ricotta, for milder flavor), grated, at room temperature
½ teaspoon paprika
⅛ teaspoon cayenne pepper
Nonstick cooking spray

continued

MAKES 6 TO 8 SERVINGS

1 Bring water to a boil in a heavy large saucepan over high heat. Add salt and stir, then sprinkle in polenta, stirring constantly. Turn heat to low, and simmer, stirring often, until thick. Grits will be tender and edges of the grains will look translucent.

2 Toss Gouda with paprika and pepper. Sprinkle the seasoned cheese by the quarter-cup into polenta, stirring with each addition.

3 Scrape the cooked polenta into a buttered or oiled 8x8x2-in. glass baking dish. Cool for 20 minutes until set, and cut into squares. Mist a skillet placed over medium heat with nonstick cooking spray. Use a broad spatula to lift the polenta squares into the hot skillet and toast both sides. Serve toasted polenta with sweet onion marmalade and strawberry salsa.

continued

Pairing: Serve with a pilsner or kellerweis bier to provide refreshing contrast to the savory onion and salsa. The noble hops will meld with the citrus flavors in the garnishes.

CHEESE POLENTA WITH SWEET ONION MARMALADE & STRAWBERRY SALSA CONTINUED

STRAWBERRY SALSA

- ¾ cup chopped fresh strawberries
- 1 diced avocado (about 1 cup)
- ¼ cup chopped fresh cilantro leaves
- ¼ cup chopped mint leaves
- 2 teaspoons lime juice
- Pinch salt
- ½ teaspoon hot pepper sauce, if desired

4 Mix strawberries, avocado, cilantro, mint, lime juice and salt in a medium glass bowl.

5 Taste and add more lime juice and hot pepper sauce if desired. Serve as garnish with polenta and onion marmalade.

MAKES 2 CUPS SALSA

SWEET ONION MARMALADE

- 2 tablespoons butter or vegetable oil
- 2 cups diced sweet onion
- 2 tablespoons minced shallots
- Juice of one orange (about ½ cup)
- ¼ teaspoon balsamic vinegar
- Pinch salt

6 Place butter or oil in a heavy, nonstick skillet over low heat. Add onion and shallots and cook until translucent. Add orange juice, vinegar and salt. Cook and stir over low heat until caramelized and thick.

MAKES 1½ CUPS

MASCARPONE FRENCH TOAST

PHOTO: MICHAEL WESSEL

MASCARPONE FRENCH TOAST

Mascarpone makes a sweet topping for fresh raspberries and French toast. Decadent with a beer-mosa for brunch!

- 4 ounces Mascarpone cheese
- ¼ cup tangerine or orange juice
- 1 to 2 tablespoons powdered sugar or maple sugar, as needed
- 4 large eggs
- 1 cup whole milk
- ½ cup half-and-half
- 2 tablespoons white sugar
- 1 teaspoon vanilla extract
- 1 teaspoon ground cinnamon
- ½ teaspoon ground nutmeg
- Pinch salt
- 8 slices challah or rustic bread (sliced about ¾-inch thick)
- 2 tablespoons butter or nonstick cooking spray
- 1 cup raspberries, rinsed and drained
- Maple syrup

1 In a small bowl, blend Mascarpone cheese, juice and a little powdered sugar or maple sugar, if the tangerine or orange juice is very tart. Add sugar by the teaspoonful, and taste, until desired sweetness is reached.

2 In a large 15x10x2-in. baking dish, whisk together the eggs, milk, half-and-half, white sugar, vanilla extract, cinnamon, nutmeg and salt. Whisk until smooth.

3 Arrange challah to soak up egg blend in baking dish. After 2 minutes, turn slices to soak on both sides. Let bread absorb the mixture, about 15 minutes. (You may need to do this in batches.)

4 Place a large skillet or griddle over medium-high heat, and spray with nonstick cooking spray or butter. If using butter, swirl around pan to coat evenly. Use a spatula to lift the softened slices of challah onto skillet or griddle, and cook about 3 minutes on each side. The bread will brown and puff as it cooks; make sure butter doesn't burn. Add more butter if needed. Place 4 serving plates in a warm 250°F oven.

5 Place 2 slices French toast on each warmed serving plate; top with one or two tablespoons Mascarpone mixture and ¼ cup raspberries, and plenty of maple syrup.

MAKES 4 SERVINGS

Pairing: Serve with a raspberry ale and orange juice beer-mosa or a tart apricot wheat ale.

SWEET POTATO GNOCCHI WITH ASIAGO

PHOTO: MICHAEL WESSEL

SWEET POTATO GNOCCHI WITH ASIAGO

1 Preheat oven to 425°F. Cut sweet potatoes in half, lengthwise, and place, cut side up, on nonstick baking sheet. Roast 60 to 90 minutes or until completely tender and oozing caramelized sugars. Remove from oven and let cool to lukewarm. Scoop out cooked potato, and place in a large bowl; discard skins. Let cool completely. Mash and measure 2 cups mashed sweet potato (reserve any extra for Zucchi Rolls, page 165.

2 Beat eggs in a mixing cup, and add to mashed sweet potato. Sift corn flour, corn starch, baking soda, salt, cinnamon and cayenne into a medium bowl. Add flour mixture by the half cupful to the mashed potatoes, just enough to make a soft dough (use more corn flour as needed to make a soft, pliable dough). Divide dough into 6 pieces, and roll each piece into a ball. Using corn flour as needed to keep dough from sticking, and roll each ball into a long rope. Cut the dough ropes into one-inch pieces. Toss with corn flour to keep from sticking and let air-dry for 30 minutes.

3 Bring a large pot of water to a boil. Drop the gnocchi into the boiling water, without crowding pot. When they float to the top, about a minute, use a slotted spoon to remove and set aside on a parchment-lined baking sheet.

4 Melt butter over medium-low heat in a large, deep skillet. Add the shallots; sauté until tender, 1-2 minutes. Add gnocchi and cook, turning once, until toasted on all sides and hot. Sprinkle with grated Asiago cheese and season with salt and pepper to taste.

2 large sweet potatoes (about 1 ½ pounds)
2 large eggs
1½ cups corn flour (or all-purpose flour), plus more for dusting and rolling
⅓ cup corn starch
½ teaspoon baking soda
1 teaspoon salt
¼ teaspoon cinnamon
¼ teaspoon cayenne
4 tablespoons unsalted butter
2 tablespoons minced shallots
½ cup grated Asiago cheese
Kosher or sea salt, to taste
Freshly ground black pepper, to taste

Pairing: Serve with American amber ale or Oktoberfest, for malty complement to the browned butter and sharp Asiago cheese flavors.

MAKES 4 SERVINGS

GORGONZOLA-STUFFED PORTOBELLO MUSHROOMS

PHOTO: MICHAEL WESSE

GORGONZOLA-STUFFED PORTOBELLO MUSHROOMS

- ¼ cup plus 2 tablespoons olive oil
- 2 cloves garlic, minced
- 2 tablespoons freshly chopped thyme leaves
- 4 ounces roasted red peppers, cut into strips, about 1 cup
- 6 large portobello mushroom caps, stems removed
- 3 tablespoons toasted bread crumbs
- 4 ounces crumbled Gorgonzola
- ½ teaspoon kosher salt
- ½ teaspoon freshly ground black pepper

1 Preheat a gas or charcoal grill to medium-high heat, or if grill is not available, preheat oven to 400°F.

2 In a medium 9-inch skillet, heat 2 tablespoons oil over medium-high heat. Add garlic and turn heat to low; add thyme and roasted red pepper strips. Cook and stir 2 minutes or until garlic is tender, and remove from heat.

3 Place mushroom caps, stem side up, on a foil baking sheet. Sprinkle with toasted bread crumbs (one to two teaspoons per mushroom). Top each cap evenly with the red pepper and garlic mixture. Top with crumbled Gorgonzola and sprinkle with salt and pepper. Place the foil sheet on grill; cover and cook until mushrooms are heated through and the cheese melts, about 5-10 minutes depending on thickness of the mushrooms, or bake in oven, on a baking sheet, until mushrooms are hot and cheese bubbling.

MAKES 6 SERVINGS

Pairing: Serve with barrel-aged brown ale or sour brown ale as a counterpoint to the earthy and salty flavors of the mushroom and Gorgonzola.

MEXICAN CORN
WITH COTIJA SAUCE

PHOTO: JENNIFER MAR

MEXICAN CORN WITH COTIJA SAUCE

1 Working with one ear of corn at a time, peel back the husks to expose the kernels, leaving husks attached at the base. Remove the corn silk and twist husks together around base of cob to form a handle. Repeat with remaining ears. Transfer corn to a large bowl or pot filled with water and soak 30 minutes.

2 Build a medium-hot fire in a charcoal grill or heat a gas grill over medium-high heat. Place corn cob on grill, with husk handles away from direct flame; cook, turning occasionally, until charred and cooked through, about 20 minutes. Remove corn from grill and brush each ear with about 1 tablespoon mayonnaise. Place cheese on a plate and roll each ear of corn in cheese to coat. Sprinkle corn evenly with some of the cilantro, ancho chile powder, and salt and pepper, pressing the corn so that seasonings and cheese will adhere to the mayonnaise. Serve with lime wedges.

MAKES 4 SERVINGS

4 large ears corn, with husks still attached

4 tablespoons mayonnaise or Vegenaise

1 cup crumbled Cotija cheese

4 tablespoons minced fresh cilantro

2 teaspoons ancho chile powder

Kosher salt and freshly ground black pepper, to taste

1 lime, cut into four wedges

Pairing: Serve with a farmhouse ale or unfiltered golden ale, as the yeasty character harmonizes with the caramelized corn and chile spices.

EGGPLANT AND BREAD CHEESE STACKS

A lovely presentation for appetizers or sandwiches, these eggplant and bread cheese stacks are full of salty umami flavors from the kalamata pesto. This recipe is adapted from chef Ulrich Kobestein, formerly of the Kohler American Club resort.

PESTO

- **1 cup kalamata olives, pitted**
- **¾ cup (2 ounces) Parmesan cheese, grated**
- **2 tablespoons toasted pine nuts or walnuts**
- **2 tablespoons olive oil**
- **1 teaspoon garlic, minced**

EGGPLANT

- **¼ cup all-purpose flour**
- **½ teaspoon kosher salt**
- **½ teaspoon freshly ground black pepper**
- **1 medium Italian eggplant, cut lengthwise into ¼-inch slices**
- **½ to 1 cup olive oil**
- **1 large loaf focaccia or round flat bread**
- **4 tomatoes, thinly sliced**
- **2 roasted red peppers, peeled, seeded and sliced**
- **11 ounces (1 package) Wisconsin Bread cheese or other Juustoleipa cheese, cut in thick slices**

1. In food processor, purée olives, Parmesan cheese, nuts, olive oil and garlic until smooth; set aside.

2. Heat oven to 400°F. Combine flour, salt and pepper in shallow plate. Coat each eggplant slice with seasoned flour. In a large skillet, heat ¼ cup of olive oil over medium-high heat. Fry eggplant slices until golden brown on both sides, adding more oil as needed. Fry in batches if necessary. Remove eggplant from skillet; blot lightly on paper towels.

3. Cut focaccia in half horizontally; spread pesto on both cut sides. Arrange eggplant slices on focaccia. Layer tomatoes, roasted peppers and bread cheese over the eggplant.

4. Place stuffed bread on large baking sheet. Bake 20 to 30 minutes or until the cheese is melted and gooey. Cut each half into 3 sandwiches. Serve warm.

MAKES 4 TO 6 SERVINGS

Pairing: Try an American porter that's dry enough to balance the acidity of the tomatoes and fried eggplant.

Estabrook Park Beer Garden MILWAUKEE, WISCONSIN

Milwaukeeans can once again say "Prost!" in a public park, at the Estabrook Park Beer Garden.

Milwaukee's beer barons built the city with profits made from malt, hops and fresh water from Lake Michigan and its nearby rivers. Old postcards of the late 19th and early 20th centuries depict a Milwaukee home with three taps in every kitchen sink: one for hot water, one for cold, and the biggest for beer.

Read any history of Milwaukee and you'll find stories of historic beer gardens established along the Milwaukee River beginning in the 19th century and continuing through Prohibition.

Remember that by 1893, the Pabst Brewing Co. became the first brewer in America to sell more than one million barrels of beer in a single year. At that time, almost one third of Milwaukee's population came from Germany, and many brought with them the desire for gemütlichkeit.

What is gemütlichkeit? It's a feeling, a state of being, and an experience all in one. It's the blend of being relaxed, happy, and peaceful while belonging and being part of public festivities in a social group. But beer gardens, and a lot of Milwaukee's brewing culture, vanished with Prohibition.

Now, after decades of private beer gardens being attached to restaurants, the Milwaukee County Department of Parks, Recreation and Culture has embraced beer gardens for the public. The Estabrook Park Beer Garden is on the Oak Leaf Trail, used by walkers, runners and bicyclists traveling near the banks of the Milwaukee River as it winds from downtown and along the east side of the city.

"German immigrants got it right when they chose beer gardens as their community gathering spaces," says Lori Fredrich, co-founder of MKEFoodies and food writer for OnMilwaukee.com. "After all, there isn't a more perfect place to spend a late summer afternoon than the beer garden, with picnics beneath century-old shade trees, a nice selection of German-style brews, and the sound of the river cascading through the park."

Tall banners for Hofbräu beckon visitors to the entryway of the park. Beer garden operations are contracted with local restaurateur Hans

PHOTOS: MICHAEL WESSEL

Weissgerber III. Weekends at Estabrook often include live music, accordions and polka bands such as the Squeezettes. You can bring your own food, or munch on pretzels with obatzter, a blend of brie and cream cheese.

Draft beer is served in heavy glass steins rented from the garden, cash only. Hofbräu beer is featured, Original, Hefe Weizen, Dunkel, and a rotating specialty draft, such as the local Lakefront Riverwest Stein lager. The beer is cold, topped with foam and served in half-liters and full liters only. There's also wine, soft drinks and a few other snacks.

Yet the main point is gemütlichkeit, enjoying your time outdoors, in the company of friends, visitors and families, while relaxing with a beverage. Mike Brenner, founder of Brenner Brewing Co., says, "While in Germany working to get my Master Brewer diploma, I spent a lot of time 'studying' in Bavarian beer gardens, and Estabrook is as authentic as I've seen in the U.S."

I am so grateful that the Milwaukee Parks System permitted me to take food photos for this cookbook at many of their picnic sites throughout the parks. Thank you and enjoy the gemütlichkeit of life in the beer garden!

—L.S.

CHAPTER 4
EGGS

RED PEPPER-TOMATO BAKED EGGS

PHOTO: MICHAEL WESSE

RED PEPPER-TOMATO BAKED EGGS

Based on a Middle Eastern specialty, shakshuka, which I first sampled at Tasty N Sons, Portland, OR, a diner famous for its menu of savory egg dishes. Choose the largest diameter peppers so the eggs cook in place.

- 1 tablespoon vegetable oil, plus more as needed
- 2 large orange or green bell peppers, at least 4 inches diameter stemmed, seeded, and cut into ¾-inch thick rings (to yield 6 rings)
- ½ cup chopped sweet onion
- 1 tablespoon minced garlic
- 1 teaspoon turmeric
- 1 teaspoon smoked paprika
- 1 teaspoon hot pepper sauce (I use Cholula)
- 1 28-oz. can tomato puree
- 1 large red bell pepper, (about 8 ounces) stemmed, seeded and diced
- 6 large eggs
- Salt and black pepper to taste
- Chopped flat leaf parsley and chives, to garnish

1 Heat oil in a very large ovenproof skillet (about 16 or 17 in. diameter; cast iron is best) over medium-low heat. Place bell pepper slices in skillet, and brown on both sides. Do this in batches so rings maintain their round shape. Set aside. Add onion and garlic to skillet, with a bit more oil if needed, and cook 3-5 minutes, stirring often, until onions soften. Add turmeric, smoked paprika, pepper sauce and tomato puree. Cook until simmering, then add diced red bell pepper. Cook, stirring occasionally, for 20 minutes or under red peppers are tender.

2 Heat oven to 350°F. Place the browned pepper rings on the surface of the hot tomato-pepper sauce. Crack an egg into a large nonstick spoon and slide the raw egg into the center of the pepper ring, pressing down a bit with the base of the spoon so egg stays in the ring. Repeat with remaining peppers and eggs.

3 Place the skillet in the top rack of the oven, and bake until eggs are cooked, about 8 to 10 minutes. Season with salt and pepper, sprinkle with chopped parsley and chives, and serve in large bowls.

MAKES 6 SERVINGS

Pairing: With the spicy, acidic tomato and pepper sauce, choose a sprightly Vienna or Oktoberfest lager or Irish red ale—a beer with malty flavors will be a toasty counterpoint to the egg's thick, sulphury yolks.

TRIO OF DEVILED EGGS

Inspired by a deviled egg feast devised for Philly Beer Week, here are three recipes that will make an appetizing assortment for brunch or bar snacks, especially when paired with a hoppy pilsner or pale ale.

CURRIED DEVILED EGGS WITH CARROT AND CORIANDER

- 6 extra-large eggs, hard boiled, halved with yolks separated into a small bowl
- 2 tablespoons mayonnaise or Vegenaise
- ½ teaspoon powdered mustard
- 1 teaspoon hot curry powder
- 1 teaspoon lemon juice
- 2 tablespoons grated carrot
- Salt and pepper, to taste
- Cilantro leaves, to garnish

1 Blend the egg yolks in a small bowl with Vegenaise, mustard, curry, lemon juice, grated carrot and salt and pepper to taste. Fill egg halves, and garnish with fresh cilantro leaves.

HORSERADISH DEVILED EGGS WITH FRIED ONIONS

- 2 ounces (wt) Walla Walla onion or white end of large leek
- 2 ounces (fl) vegetable oil
- 6 extra-large eggs, hard boiled, halved with yolks separated into a small bowl
- 2 tablespoons mayonnaise or Vegenaise
- 1 teaspoon fresh grated horseradish
- ½ teaspoon Dijon mustard
- Salt and pepper to taste

1 Chop the onion or leek into thin slivers. Heat oil in a nonstick skillet over medium high heat. Add onion or leek and fry until golden and crispy. Remove fried onions from skillet and set aside to drain on paper towel or parchment paper. Mix egg yolk in a small bowl with Vegenaise, horseradish, and Dijon mustard. Fill the egg halves with blend and garnish with fried onions or slivered leeks, and salt and pepper.

TRIO OF DEVILED EGGS CONTINUED

SRIRACHA DEVILED EGGS

- **6 extra-large eggs, hard boiled, halved with yolks separated out into a bowl**
- **2 tablespoons mayonnaise or Vegenaise**
- **1 tablespoon Sriracha (Vietnamese chili sauce)**
- **1 teaspoon lime juice**
- **2 tablespoons minced daikon radish**
- **Salt and cayenne pepper to taste**

Pairing: I suggest a trio of pale ales, from American, Belgian and English breweries, to compare and contrast. A bready Continental pilsner would also be refreshing.

1 Mix egg yolks in a small bowl with Vegenaise, Sriracha, lime juice and minced daikon radish, seasoned to taste with salt and dust lightly with cayenne pepper.

ARRANGE EGGS ON LARGE PLATTER—
MAKES 12 SERVINGS
(3 DEVILED EGGS PER PERSON)

OMELET WITH SHIITAKE MUSHROOMS

PHOTO: MICHAEL WESS

OMELET WITH SHIITAKE MUSHROOMS

If you make the hollandaise sauce on page 68, you'll be ready to use the leftover egg whites in this tasty omelet.

- 1 tablespoon vegetable oil
- 2 teaspoons unsalted butter, divided
- 5 medium-sized shiitake mushrooms, stemmed, sliced thinly
- 2 tablespoons minced shallots
- 1 cup diced mixed red, yellow and green bell peppers
- 1 teaspoon minced garlic
- ½ teaspoon minced thyme
- ½ teaspoon tamari or soy sauce
- 3 large eggs
- 2 large egg whites
- Kosher salt, to taste
- Freshly ground black pepper, to taste
- Finely chopped fresh parsley, for garnish

1 In a 9-inch nonstick skillet over medium-high heat, melt oil and 1 teaspoon butter. Stir in mushrooms, shallots, diced bell peppers, and garlic. Cook, stirring occasionally, until the mushrooms begin to turn golden brown and peppers are crisp-tender, 4 to 5 minutes. Sprinkle with minced thyme and tamari.

2 Remove from heat and scrape vegetable mixture onto a warm plate. Whisk together eggs and egg whites in a medium bowl.

3 Place the same nonstick skillet back over medium-high heat and add the remaining teaspoon of butter. Use a heat-proof spatula to coat the pan, and add the beaten eggs. Swirl the pan to spread eggs evenly, and gently lift edges as the omelet cooks, tilting the pan so that raw egg mixture will flow underneath onto the hot pan and cook evenly.

4 When eggs are set, spread the warm pepper mixture evenly in the center of the omelet, and fold over the eggs. Slide the omelet onto a warm plate and sprinkle with parsley and salt and pepper to taste.

MAKES 2 SERVINGS

Pairing: Try a beer-mosa made with orange juice and Weiss bier or American wheat ale. Or make a savory Michelada with a splash of tomato juice, fresh lemon and Rogue Chipotle Ale or a spicy chili beer of your choice.

TOMATO EGGS BENEDICT WITH HOLLANDAISE

PHOTO: MICHAEL WESSEL

TOMATO EGGS BENEDICT WITH HOLLANDAISE

When tomatoes are lush and ripe, their sweetness counters the mineral flavors of spinach and sulphur edge in egg yolks. I make the hollandaise sauce in a blender first, prepare the vegetables, and simultaneously poach the eggs and toast the muffins. Have warm plates at the ready, or serve in a pre-warmed ceramic dish that will keep the eggs warm until serving.

TOMATO EGGS BENEDICT

5 cups boiling water, divided

1 teaspoon white or malt vinegar

4 ounces fresh baby spinach, cleaned, stemmed and chopped

2 large ripe tomatoes, about 4 inches in diameter

4 large eggs

2 English muffins, split in half

2 tablespoons softened butter

Blender hollandaise, recipe, page 68

Paprika, salt and pepper, to taste

1 Bring 3 cups water and vinegar to a simmer in a large 10 or 12-inch nonstick skillet, over medium-high heat. Boil 2 cups water and pour slowly over baby spinach in a colander to wilt them; let drain. Slice tomatoes into half-inch thick slices, and choose 4 slices that most closely fit the diameter of the muffins. Set aside.

2 Turn heat off after skillet water comes to a simmer. Crack an egg into a large ladle and gently slide the egg into the hot water. Repeat with remaining eggs, try to keep them from sticking together. Cover skillet and let eggs steep in the hot water for 4-5 minutes for soft yolks, 8 minutes for firm yolks. Meanwhile, toast and butter the English muffin halves. Assemble the eggs Benedict as quickly as possible, topping the hot buttered muffin with drained baby spinach, a tomato slice, poached egg and top with hollandaise as desired. Sprinkle with paprika, salt and pepper.

continued

MAKES 4 SERVINGS (ONE EGG PER PERSON)

TOMATO EGGS BENEDICT WITH HOLLANDAISE CONTINUED

There are several versions of blender hollandaise, including recipes by Julia Child and Marion Cunningham. This recipe is adapted from Cunningham's BREAKFAST BOOK, (Knopf, 1987) to use pasteurized eggs and a stick blender, and whips up in 10 minutes.

BLENDER HOLLANDAISE

3 large pasteurized egg yolks, whisked
2 tablespoons boiling water
1 cup hot, freshly melted butter (2 sticks)
2 tablespoons freshly squeezed lemon juice
Pinch celery salt
Pinch cayenne pepper

Pairing: A creamy Kölsch beer makes an ideal pairing for the toasted bread and lemony hollandaise sauce. Its sweet character and effervescence cuts through the acidity of the tomato and mineral flavors of the spinach.

1 Because raw or undercooked eggs may cause health problems, you may wish to use pasteurized eggs to make this sauce. Start by washing the whole eggs still in their shells in hot soapy water. Rinse and place in a saucepan and cover the eggs with fresh water with 1 teaspoon baking soda added. Place on stovetop and use an instant-read thermometer to track the temperature. Turn heat to HIGH and bring water to 140°F. Keep water hot at 140°F for 3 minutes (and no higher than 142°F), turning burner heat down to MEDIUM if needed. Remove eggs from hot water and rinse with cold water. Shell the eggs and make the recipe immediately. *While this technique reduces the risk of salmonella, no one who is ill, elderly, very young, or pregnant women, should eat raw eggs.*

2 Put the egg yolks in a tall thermal mug (at least 22 oz.) with a base wide enough to fit the blade assembly of the stick blender. Pulse for a few seconds with stick blender, then slowly drizzle in boiling water, while pulsing stick blender. Drizzle in hot butter, almost one drop of butter at a time to hold the emulsion, while pulsing stick blender. Add the lemon juice, celery salt and a pinch of cayenne pepper, and pulse to blend. The sauce will hold its emulsion for at several hours. Re-blend with a bit more hot water and a bit more lemon juice if it seems too thick.

MAKES 1 CUP SAUCE

BABY SPINACH, MUSHROOM & PEPPER CUP EGGS

PHOTO: MICHAEL WESSEL

BABY SPINACH, MUSHROOM & PEPPER CUP EGGS

- ¼ cup malt vinegar
- ¼ cup olive oil
- 1 tablespoon Dijon mustard
- 1 teaspoon lemon juice
- 1 teaspoon brown sugar
- 1 teaspoon celery seed
- ¼ teaspoon ground coriander
- ⅛ teaspoon ground white pepper
- 1 teaspoon salt
- 3 ounces small white mushrooms, washed and sliced (about ⅔ cup)
- 3 ounces baby spinach, washed and stemmed (about 1 cup, packed)
- 1 yellow bell pepper, stemmed, at least 4 inches in diameter
- 2½ teaspoons butter, divided
- 1 beaten egg
- 2 large eggs
- Fresh minced parsley, to garnish

1 In a large nonstick skillet, whisk together vinegar, oil, mustard, lemon juice, brown sugar, celery seed, coriander, white pepper and salt. Place over medium heat, add mushrooms and stir until evenly coated. Cook just until mushrooms begin to release their juices. Remove from heat, scrape mushroom mixture into a glass dish and set aside. Do not clean the pan.

2 Clean and stem the baby spinach. Divide among 2 serving dishes. Slice yellow bell pepper into two ⅔ inch thick rings. Trim away any pith or seeds with a small knife.

3 Place the large nonstick skillet over medium-low heat. Melt 2 teaspoons butter in the skillet and add pepper rings. Cook on one side until edges are browned, about 2-3 minutes. Place beaten egg in a shallow rimmed dish. Use a pair of tongs to lift the pepper rings and dip the uncooked edge in the beaten egg.

continued

Substitution: For lower-oxalate diets, use baby kale or baby bok choy instead of spinach; blanch the greens in boiling water and drain well before using.

BABY SPINACH, MUSHROOM & PEPPER CUP EGGS CONTINUED

4 Place rings, egg-dipped side facing down, in skillet. Drop a dab of butter, about ¼ teaspoon, inside each of the pepper rings. Break a large egg into the center of each pepper ring, over the melted butter. Add 2 tablespoons water to base of skillet, outside the pepper rings. Cover and cook until eggs are set, about 5 to 6 minutes for soft yolks, 8 minutes for hard cooked eggs.

5 Divide spinach between two serving dishes, and top each with a spoonful of mushrooms. Top each dish with a cooked egg-pepper ring. Garnish with minced parsley.

Pairing: A spicy Biere de Garde makes a welcome contrast to the mushrooms, tangy spinach and creamy eggs.

MAKES 2 SERVINGS

BAKED EGGS WITH SWEET POTATO HASH

PHOTO: MICHAEL WESSE

BAKED EGGS WITH SWEET POTATO HASH

Supper or brunch, these baked eggs are easy to prepare, especially if you use a shortcut such as chopped frozen sweet potato French fries to make the hash. One of our favorite pubs in Milwaukee, Stubby's, makes excellent sweet potato fries served in gargantuan proportions. We take home the leftovers to make this hash at home the next morning. If using fresh sweet potatoes, cook the diced sweet potatoes in oil in a large skillet over medium heat, until tender, then proceed with the recipe.

1 tablespoon plus 1 teaspoon olive oil
1 cup diced sweet potatoes
2 tablespoons minced sweet onion
½ teaspoon sweet marjoram
2 large eggs
Salt and freshly ground black pepper, to taste

1 Preheat oven to 350°F. Place a medium skillet over medium-high heat and cook sweet potatoes in 1 tablespoon olive oil, stirring and cooking until tender, about 10 minutes. Grease 2 large ramekins (8 ounce capacity) with the remaining oil. Toss the minced onion with the cooked, diced sweet potatoes and marjoram, and divide evenly between two ramekins.

2 Place ramekins on a baking sheet and bake 10 minutes or until potatoes are hot. Remove the pan from the oven, break an egg over each ramekin and return to the oven to cook the eggs, about 10 to 12 minutes. Season with salt and pepper.

MAKES 2 SERVINGS

Pairing: A coffee stout will pick up the sweetness of the potato hash, and make a toasty contrast to the herb flavors.

TORTILLA CUP EGGS WITH GUACAMOLE

PHOTO: MICHAEL WESSEL

TORTILLA CUP EGGS WITH GUACAMOLE

My grandmother loved testing new recipes, and one of her finds in the 1950s was her quaintly spelled "Quacamole," a mash-up of avocado, lime juice, onion, garlic and chili powder. Baked in corn tortilla shells, the eggs and avocados make a portable feast for brunch.

- 6 small flour or corn tortillas (6-in. diameter)
- Nonstick cooking spray
- 1½ cups "Quacamole" (recipe below)
- 6 large eggs
- Hot pepper sauce
- Crumbled Cotiija cheese
- ½ teaspoon paprika

1 Preheat oven to 350°F. One at a time, warm the corn tortillas in a skillet over medium-low heat. Spray the interior of a 6 cup muffin tray. Press a warm tortilla into muffin tray using a small (4 ounce) glass custard cup or a wooden spoon. Repeat with remaining tortillas.

2 Place 1 tablespoon guacamole in the base of each tortilla cup. Break an egg into each tortilla cup and bake 20 minutes or until eggs are set. Garnish edges of tortilla cups with more guacamole, and serve with hot pepper sauce, crumbled Cotija cheese and paprika.

MARGERY BUDD'S"QUACAMOLE"

GUACAMOLE

- 1 teaspoon minced garlic
- 2 tablespoons minced onion
- 1 teaspoon salt
- ¼ teaspoon ground black pepper
- ½ teaspoon chili powder (try ground chipotle for smoky edge)
- ⅛ teaspoon cayenne
- 1 tablespoon lime juice
- 1 teaspoon olive oil
- 2 ripe avocados, pitted and mashed (about 10 ounces total)

1 Mash all ingredients together. Chill at least one hour for flavors to meld.

MAKES 1 HEAPING CUP

Pairing: A Mexican dark lager or Oktoberfest makes a refreshing partner.

ARTICHOKE SALAD WITH CHOPPED EGGS

PHOTO: MICHAEL WESSEL

ARTICHOKE SALAD WITH CHOPPED EGGS

If you're lucky enough to live in California or the Pacific Northwest, it's possible to find beautiful fresh baby artichokes that aren't expensive. Here in the Midwest, I rely on frozen, quartered artichoke hearts for this easy recipe. Most package sizes range from 9 to 12 ounces in the US, so feel free to adjust the ratios of the other ingredients to match.

10 ounces fresh or frozen, thawed artichoke hearts, cut into bite-sized chunks
1 cup cooked chickpeas, drained (canned OK)
½ cup diced orange bell pepper
1 tablespoon chopped capers
½ teaspoon minced garlic
½ teaspoon grated lemon zest
3 tablespoons fresh lemon juice (½ lemon)
¼ cup olive oil
4 large eggs
Salt and ground black pepper, to taste
8 sprigs fresh basil

1 Preheat oven to 325°F. Place artichoke hearts in an even layer in a 9x13-inch glass baking dish. Sprinkle with chickpeas and bell pepper. Mix capers, garlic, lemon zest, lemon juice and olive oil. Spoon over the mixed vegetables and stir to coat evenly. Place in oven, tent dish with foil, and bake 20 to 30 minutes.

2 While artichokes bake, hard boil the whole eggs in a medium saucepan filled with water; boil for 15 minutes. Remove from heat, drain and cover with cold water to cool. When cool enough to handle, remove shells and cut eggs into quarters, lengthwise.

3 Remove the artichoke mixture from the oven, and divide among four plates. Top with the sliced eggs, season with salt and pepper, and garnish with fresh basil leaves.

MAKES 4 SERVINGS

Pairing: A brown ale will balance the competing flavors of artichokes, tart lemon, salty capers and hard-boiled eggs.

The August Schell Brewery Gardens

August Schell arrived in New Ulm, MN, in 1856, and quickly realized the potential for a brewery to be built in this enclave of German immigrants. In the fall of 1860, Schell and his partner built a small brewery just two miles from town along the banks of the Cottonwood River.

The location of the brewery was ideal. Beyond the beauty of its woodlands, the brewery site featured an artesian spring, providing pure water for brewing. The Cottonwood River became essential to the brewery's lagering refrigeration process. Each winter, large blocks of ice would be harvested and hauled up the hill where they would be stored in underground caves. The ice would keep the caves cool throughout the spring and early summer in order to allow proper aging and fermentation of the beer.

By 1885, August Schell had bought out his partner. With his wife, Theresa, he built the exquisite Schell Mansion on the brewery grounds, complete with fountains, formal gardens and a fenced deer park (all listed on the National Register of Historic Sites). The August Schell Brewing Co. is now the second oldest family owned brewery in the United States, and its brewery gardens are often the site for events and festivals.

In addition to traditional plantings along paths, the brewery garden's deer park features natural landscaping with wild ferns, grasses, and trees. Several enormous black spruce and cedars, some more than 100 years old, were planted from seeds hand-carried from Schell's former family home in Germany. A small greenhouse and hoop house accommodate the more than 60 different annuals planted in 8 formal gardens every summer.

Family mementos augment the gardens in fascinating places. Bits of ceramic bier steins are imbedded in the stonework for the 19th century fountain, along with sea shells from Schell family travels.

Now, a family of peacocks adds color and drama to strolls in the garden, as well as sightings of deer and other wildlife. Jodi and Ted Marti, with son Franz (the 5th and 6th generations of the Schell family), oversee the gardens.

The Brewery and gardens have become one of the most popular tourist destinations in Minnesota over the past 20 years. The grounds are open to the public from dawn to dusk. Whether meeting for a quiet lunch on a bench, students touring the brewery museum, or people just enjoying the gardens, Schell's proudly offers a beautiful piece of nature for all to enjoy.

"This summer, we added an outdoor Sunday Bier Garten featuring German music, beverages and a light snack," says Jodi Marti. Though the actual number of visitors to the gardens is unknown, more than 30,000 people enjoy the brewery tours each year, and the Bier Garten will be a big draw in the summers to come.

Dinner in the Beer Garden

CHAPTER 5

FISH & SEAFOOD

SHRIMP IN NAPA WRAPS WITH COCONUT-CHILE SAUCE

- 12 ounces Kölsch or American wheat ale
- ¼ cup dark toasted sesame oil
- 1 tablespoon frozen lime juice concentrate
- 2 tablespoons fish sauce
- 1 tablespoon minced garlic, or to taste
- 1 tablespoon hot Chinese powdered ginger
- 1 teaspoon powdered cardamom
- 1 teaspoon (or more to taste) Chinese red chili paste
- 1½ pounds large shelled shrimp (20 count size to yield about 30)
- 10 bamboo skewers, soaked in water 30 minutes, or a grill basket
- 10 Napa cabbage leaves, cleaned and trimmed, about 5-6 inches long

1 Blend the beer, sesame oil, lime juice concentrate, fish sauce, garlic, ginger, cardamom, and chili paste in a medium bowl and whisk well. Rinse shrimp in cold water, drain well, and place in a large nonreactive shallow dish or gallon zip-seal plastic bag. Pour in marinade, and stir so shrimp are evenly coated. Cover or seal, and refrigerate one hour, or up to overnight.

2 Preheat a grill to 350°F. Place drained shrimp in a grill basket or thread on skewers. Grill 30-40 seconds on each side, until shrimp just turn pink. The shrimp will continue to cook when you remove them from the grill, be careful not to overcook them. Grill the jalapeño for coconut sauce at this time, too.

3 Place 2 to 3 shrimp inside each Napa cabbage leaf on a large platter and serve with a spoonful of coconut-chili sauce.

COCONUT CHILE SAUCE

- 1 small green jalapeño, grilled
- 1/2 cup plain coconut cream
- 1 teaspoon red chili paste
- 1/2 teaspoon grated lime zest
- 1 tablespoon minced cilantro

COCONUT CHILE SAUCE

1 Remove stem, skin and seeds from the grilled jalapeño and mince. Blend coconut cream, jalapeño, chili paste, lime zest and minced cilantro on HIGH in a blender. Serve as a condiment with each shrimp-stuffed cabbage leaf.

MAKES ½ CUP

SMOKED TROUT SOBA NOODLES

Fresh grilled trout is also wonderful with these noodles, but as a pantry staple, I'll use a 3- to 4-ounce tin of smoked trout to make this recipe. Don't be intimidated by the long list of ingredients, as it goes together quickly, in less than 30 minutes. Soba noodles are fast cooking and the buckwheat variety adds great flavor.

- 4 ounces soba noodles
- Pinch salt
- 2 tablespoons vegetable oil
- 1 tablespoon chili sesame oil or 1 tablespoon toasted sesame oil and chili paste to taste
- 6 ounces shiitake mushrooms, cleaned, stemmed and sliced
- ¾ cup chopped red bell pepper
- ¼ cup chopped scallions (or more, to taste)
- 3.5 -4 ounce can smoked trout, drained
- 2 tablespoons rice wine vinegar
- 2 tablespoons minced ginger
- ¼ cup toasted almond slices
- 1 -2 tablespoons chopped fresh cilantro leaves
- 1 to 2 tablespoons fresh lemon juice

MAKES 2 SERVINGS

1 Bring one quart water to a boil in a 2-quart saucepan, and add soba noodles and salt. Bring to a simmer.

2 While noodles cook, place vegetable oil and chili sesame oil in a large skillet, over medium-high heat, and add mushrooms, bell pepper and scallions, stirring and cooking until just tender, about 3 minutes. Reduce heat to low.

3 Add drained smoked trout to vegetables in skillet, and add vinegar and ginger. Cook until trout is warmed through.

4 Check soba noodles for doneness, and drain. Add hot drained noodles to the large skillet, tossing so vegetables and fish are mixed in. Top with toasted almonds, cilantro and fresh squeezed lemon juice.

Pairing: A fun pairing is the Rogue Ales Morimoto Black Obi Soba Ale, which uses soba in the brew; otherwise, try a porter, to pick up the smoky edge of the trout without overwhelming the taste of the fish.

ROGUE ALES DIRTOIR WITH ASPARAGUS & DUNGENESS CRAB SALAD

PHOTO: JENNIFER MA

ASPARAGUS & DUNGENESS CRAB SALAD

The Pacific coast is a haven for seafood, and Rogue Ales' original pub in Newport Beach features plenty of seafood on the menu. This recipe is a riff on a salad served at a beer dinner at Wildwood Restaurant.

- 4 to 6 small scallions (about 3 ounces by weight)
- ¼ cup chopped fresh parsley
- ¼ cup chopped fresh dill
- 2 cloves garlic, peeled and chopped
- 2 tablesoons freshly squeezed lime juice
- 1 teaspoon kosher salt
- ½ teaspoon freshly ground black pepper
- ½ cup sour cream
- 2 ripe avocadoes, peeled and mashed (about 1 cup)
- Hot pepper sauce, to taste
- 1½ pounds asparagus, cleaned and trimmed
- 1 tablespoon olive oil
- 1 tablespoon balsamic vinegar
- 8 oz. cooked Dungeness lump crab meat, picked over and flaked
- ¼ teaspoon smoked paprika

1 Wash and trim ends of scallions. Chop scallions to yield about ¾ cup. Place in food processor fitted with metal chopping blade. Add parsley, dill, garlic, lime juice, salt, pepper, sour cream, avocado and several dashes of hot pepper sauce. Cover food processor and puree until the mixture is smooth. Place dressing in refrigerator to chill (kept covered, this can be made a day ahead).

2 Prepare grill for medium heat (about 350°F). Place asparagus spears on foil sheet or mesh grill grate and brush with olive oil and balsamic vinegar. Grill over indirect heat until tender, about 12 minutes, turning often. Asparagus may be oven roasted instead.

3 Place asparagus on serving dish and top with spoonfuls of green avocado cream, and sprinkle with salt and pepper, then top with cooked, shredded Dungeness crab meat. Sprinkle crab with smoked paprika.

MAKES 4 SERVINGS

Pairing: The grilled asparagus pairs well with Rogue Farms Dirtoir Black Lager or a schwarzbier that's not too hoppy to overwhelm the sweet briny crab flavor. The black malts accent the smoky edge of the grilled asparagus, and balance the vegetable flavors.

ROASTED TUNA NICOISE

Roasted vegetables, topped with herbed tuna, pair wonderfully with a dark lager or black beer, to heighten the roasted, caramelized flavors.

- 1½ pounds new potatoes (redskins)
- 10 ounces green beans (haricots verts)
- 8 ounces frozen artichoke hearts, thawed
- 1 cup chopped red onion
- 1 cup celery, cut into 1-inch chunks
- 2 tablespoon olive oil, divided
- Salt and freshly ground black pepper, to taste
- 2 tablespoons capers, drained
- 1 cup chopped tomatoes
- ½ cup oil-cured olives, pitted, chopped
- 2 tablespoons chopped fresh basil (1 teaspoon dried)
- 1 tablespoon chopped fresh marjoram (½ teaspoon dried)
- 2 tablespoons lemon juice
- 2 tuna filets (about 1 pound total)
- 8 ounces bibb or butter lettuce, rinsed and torn into bite-sized pieces
- 4 lemon wedges
- 2 large eggs, hard cooked, peeled and quartered
- 2 tablespoons minced parsley

1 Preheat oven to 400°F. Scrub and chop the potatoes and wash and trim the green beans into bite-sized pieces. Rinse artichoke hearts in a colander. Drain and place the cleaned vegetables in large roasting dish. Cover with onion and celery, and drizzle with 1 tablespoon olive oil. Season with salt and pepper, and sprinkle with capers. Cover dish with foil, and roast 20-25 minutes, or until a potato is almost completely tender when pierced with a fork.

2 Mix chopped tomatoes, olives, basil, marjoram, remaining olive oil and lemon juice in a small bowl. Remove pan from oven and carefully remove foil wearing oven mitts, avoiding steam. Place tuna filets on top of vegetables, and spoon the chopped tomato mixture evenly over fish. Return pan to oven, uncovered, and bake 5-10 minutes, depending on thickness of filets. Remove from oven.

3 Arrange lettuce on edges of four serving plates, and garnish each with a lemon wedge and 2 hard cooked egg slices. Divide vegetables and fish evenly between the plates. Sprinkle with parsley.

MAKES 4 SERVINGS

Pairing: A dark, malty lager or dunkel complements the vegetables and fish, without overextending the fish oil flavors.

STEAMED MUSSELS

Thanks to Chef Micheal Iles of the Sierra Nevada Brewing Co., for sharing his favorite recipe for mussels steamed in pale ale. Mussels are one of the more sustainably harvested shellfish, particularly those from Prince Edward Island, Nova Scotia, Canada. Chef Iles uses Sierra Nevada Pale Ale and their house Porter Mustard to make the sauce.

- 1 tablespoon canola oil
- 1 cup diced yellow onion
- 1 cup diced celery
- 1 tablespoon minced garlic
- 1½ cups chopped tomatoes
- ¼ cup roasted green chiles
- 1 large bay leaf
- Salt and pepper, to taste
- 2 cups pale ale
- 2 pounds mussels, scrubbed, debearded and rinsed well
- 2 tablespoons stoneground or Dijon mustard
- 2 tablespoons cream
- 2 tablespoons butter

1 Heat the canola oil in a large skillet, deep enough to hold all the mussels and fitted with a lid, over medium heat. Add onion, celery, tomatoes, garlic, chilis and bay leaf. Cook over medium heat 5 minutes, stirring occasionally to keep tomatoes from sticking.

2 Add pale ale and mussels, and increase heat to medium-high. Stir the pot well, and cover. After 2-3 minutes, remove the lid, and stir well. Cook 2-3 minutes more over high heat, covered to capture steam, then reduce heat to low. Use long-handled tongs to remove and discard any mussels that have not opened after cooking for 6 minutes.

3 Move the open, cooked mussels to a warmed serving bowl. Whisk mustard, cream and butter into the sauce in the skillet, and add more salt and pepper if needed. Pour the sauce over the mussels and serve with toasted bread.

MAKES 4 APPETIZER OR 2 FULL SERVINGS

Pairing: Sierra Nevada Pale Ale has a vibrant citrus hoppy taste to stand in for fresh lemon in the shellfish pairing.

ALASKAN BREWING CO. ALES WITH ALASKAN SALMON & SPICY SLAW

PHOTO: JENNIFER MAR

ALASKAN SALMON WITH SPICY SLAW

Both recipes are by Tom West who has been with the Alaskan Brewing Co. since 1987, and is a perennial winner of the company's Brew Crew Cook-Off each November.

ALASKAN AMBER GLAZED SALMON

- ¼ cup Alaskan Amber ale
- 4 tablespoons butter
- 2 tablespoons honey
- 1 tablespoon lemon juice
- 1 tablespoon soy sauce
- 1 teaspoon ground cumin
- 1 teaspoon lemon pepper
- 2 pounds Wild Alaska salmon or halibut

1 Combine all ingredients except fish in small saucepot. Bring to a boil over medium-high heat, turn to low to simmer 10-15 minutes. Remove from heat and cool. May be made in advance and refrigerated until ready to use.

2 Coat fish with glaze and grill or bake at 450°F basting frequently, for 5-7 minutes for salmon, or 10-15 minutes for halibut, depending on thickness of fish. Serve with slaw, recipe follows.

continued

MAKES 6 SERVINGS

Note: Alaskan salmon, particularly Copper River salmon that's fresh caught, has a brilliant oily sheen that can coat the palate. The lemony beer glaze balances the natural fish oil and makes the pairing harmonize.

Pairing: Alaskan Summer Ale has a soft finish with a hint of wheat malt and ripe apricots from the yeast esters, making it a refreshing foil to the glazed grilled salmon. If you prefer a maltier finish, try the salmon with Alaskan Amber Ale, which has a toffee-apple malt body, accented with noble hops to raise the perceived heat index of the spicy slaw.

ALASKAN SALMON WITH SPICY SLAW CONTINUED

SPICY COLESLAW

- 1 small head green cabbage, shredded
- 1 cup chopped walnuts
- ¾ cup mayonnaise
- ¼ cup red wine vinegar
- 3 tablespoons prepared Dijon mustard
- 2 teaspoons garlic powder
- 1 teaspoon ground cayenne pepper

3 Combine cabbage and walnuts. In a small bowl, whisk together remaining ingredients. Pour mayonnaise mixture over cabbage mixture. Stir until well blended.

4 Cover and refrigerate 2 to 3 hours to allow flavors to blend.

5 Store in an airtight container in the refrigerator until ready to serve.

PHOTO: JENNIFER MARX

MALT-SEARED SCALLOPS WITH CELERY-PEAR CREAM

I like the sweetness of pears and crunchy celery paired with these malt-crusted seared scallops. If you don't have chocolate barley malt on hand, you can substitute 1 tablespoon finely ground espresso.

- **1 tablespoon minced shallot or sweet onion**
- **¼ cup heavy cream**
- **1 peeled and chopped ripe Anjou or Bartlett pear (about ½ cup)**
- **¼ cup minced celery**
- **4 tablespoons unsalted butter, cut into small cubes**
- **1 tablespoon powdered chocolate malt**
- **½ teaspoon kosher salt**
- **12 to 16 large sea scallops, cleaned and drained**
- **½ teaspoon grated orange zest**
- **1 tablespoon minced parsley**

1 In a small saucepan, simmer shallot and cream until tender, about 2 minutes over medium-low heat. Stir in chopped pear and celery, and stir. Turn heat to very low to keep sauce warm. Meanwhile, place four small (6 to 8 inches diameter) serving plates in a 200°F oven to keep warm.

2 Place butter in a large heavy skillet, and heat over medium-high heat until butter melts. Mix powdered chocolate malt and kosher salt on a plate. Dip one flat side of each sea scallop in malted salt, lightly pressing the mixture in place. Cook scallops, starting malt crust side down, 2 to 3 minutes on both sides, with cooking time depending on thickness, about 4 minutes total for scallops that are 1-inch thick. Do not overcook scallops as they will continue to cook for a few minutes after plating.

3 Place 2 tablespoons pear and celery mixture on each of the warmed plates, and top with 3 or 4 scallops per plate. Mix orange zest and parsley; sprinkle over scallops. Serve immediately.

MAKES 4 SERVINGS

Pairing: Black wheat ale, or American Imperial wheat ale—a black wheat ale will accent the malt crust on the scallop, or an Imperial wheat ale can meld with the citrus zest garnish and cut through the creamy pear sauce.

New Glarus Brewing Co.

THE HILLTOP BEER GARDEN, NEW GLARUS, WI

PHOTO: S

Husband and wife team, Dan and Deb Carey began the New Glarus Brewery with just an old abandoned warehouse and used milk tanks. Early on, they made a deliberate decision to honor the local vernacular as the brewery grew beyond its humble beginning. Both the original Riverside location and the newer Hilltop Brewery reflect Old World traditions in both brewing and architecture.

As a Wisconsin native, New Glarus Brewing Co. Founder and President Deb Carey sticks to her roots selling her husband Dan's award-winning brews sold "Only in Wisconsin." As one of the few Diploma Master Brewers in America, Dan is respected not only for the quality of his beers but also for his innovation in brewing. Dan's Wisconsin Belgian Red cherry ale was inducted into the Slow Food Ark as the first soured fruit beer brewed outside of Belgium. Pioneering New Glarus has been aging beers in oak and souring beers since the brewery's beginning in 1993.

New Glarus Brewing Co.'s Riverside location nestles into the north end of the Village. Their original copper kettle brewery is now home to

PHOTO: ZACH HEISE

America's first Wild Fruit Cave dedicated to sour spontaneously fermented beers. Dan regularly treats fans to Berliner Weiss, a selection of Belgian Sour and Brown Ales. New Glarus is known for stellar fruit beers like Raspberry Tart, Serendipity and Strawberry Rhubarb. The coolship can be viewed through the ground level windows. Wooden tanks and barrel-aged beers are housed in the cave, complete with a living turf grass roof.

As you meander up the winding drive to Hilltop Brewery, on the south edge of the Village, you'll pass a small trellised hop garden across from a small red barn that houses the state of the art wastewater treatment facility. The brewery's cellar pays homage to the neighboring farmers, utilizing a gigantic red barn structure to house the fermenters for the Wisconsin favorite farmhouse ale, Spotted Cow.

The grounds surrounding the brewery are literally carved into the hillside from the natural limestone escarpment that forms the Hilltop's stone steps. The Tasting Room's courtyard features timbered beams covered with hops, linking the hillside walking paths to the Folly.

What is a Folly? A Folly is a whimsical garden feature, designed to look like ruins that become a focal point. The New Glarus Brewery Follies

invoke a brewery from years past, with a Malt House and Bottle Shop to capture a visitor's imagination. The Folly and its meandering paths now delight over 150,000 visitors to the Wisconsin brewery in every season.

The Folly is built of stone, 100-year-old brick and heavy timbers, providing beauty and inviting exploration even in snowy winter months. Visitors enjoy free self-guided tours and tastings year round.

Visitor Zach Heise says, "I loved looking out from the hilltop beer pavilion at the rolling farm fields and forests below us—combined with the pretty "ruins" surrounding us, it was like being the lord of a castle!" ■

Dinner in the Beer Garden

CHAPTER 6

GREENS

ENDIVE WITH ORANGES, PISTACHIOS AND PARMESAN CREAM

PHOTO: JENNIFER MAR

ENDIVE WITH ORANGES, PISTACHIOS & PARMESAN CREAM

- 6 white endives (about 3 ounces each)
- Salt and freshly ground black pepper
- Extra virgin olive oil
- 2 sweet oranges, peeled and segmented
- 2 tablespoons chopped toasted pistachios
- ½ cup Mascarpone or sour cream or plain Greek yogurt
- ¼ cup Parmesan cheese
- 2 teaspoons minced chives
- ½ teaspoon orange zest
- 2 teaspoons white balsamic vinegar

1 Preheat the grill or barbecue to medium heat. Wash and trim the endives and remove any bruised outer leaves. Slice endives in half lengthwise if small, or, if very large, slice lengthwise into fourths.

2 Brush them lightly with oil on all sides and sprinkle with salt and pepper. Grill endives over a medium fire, turning them a few times, until they are lightly golden and soft on all sides, about 10 minutes. Arrange endives on a serving platter, cutting off any tips that may have gotten too charred. Arrange oranges on top. Sprinkle with toasted pistachios.

3 Mix Mascarpone or sour cream or Greek yogurt, Parmesan cheese, chives, orange zest, white balsamic vinegar and salt and pepper to taste. Serve with grilled endive.

MAKES 4-6 SERVINGS AS APPETIZER OR SIDE SALAD.

Pairing: The smoky edge of the grilled endive is highlighted with a dry American porter, savory with the creamy, salty flavors of the cheese dressing. Alaskan Brewing Co. smoked porter, Deschutes Black Butte Porter or New Glarus Porter are good examples.

RADICCHIO SALAD WITH TOASTED PECANS

Radicchio are vibrant, crunchy, and just slightly bitter, a wonderful foil to sweet apples and toasted spiced pecans. The recipe is versatile, and you can use daikon radish instead of celery for extra crunch.

- **10 to 12 ounces radicchio**
- **2 small Granny Smith green apples (about 8 ounces)**
- **One half lemon**
- **1 teaspoon salt**
- **1 cup sliced celery**
- **1 teaspoon Dijon mustard**
- **1 tablespoon raw honey**
- **2 tablespoons extra-virgin olive oil**
- **¼ teaspoon ground white pepper**
- **¼ teaspoon powdered ginger**
- **½ cup toasted pecans (halves or pieces)**

MAKES 4 SERVINGS

1 Clean and trim off the woody ends and cores of the radicchio. Slice in half lengthwise, and then slice again into quarters. Slice or shred into bite-sized pieces and place in a large salad bowl.

2 Wash, core, and slice the apples into bite-sized wedges, and add to the radicchio. Sprinkle the apples and radicchio with lemon juice and salt, and toss. Add celery.

3 Mix the mustard, honey and olive oil in a small saucepan over medium heat until honey is well emulsified. Toss the warm dressing with the radicchio salad.

4 Mix pepper and ginger, and toss with ½ cup toasted pecans. If desired, add one teaspoon sugar. Sprinkle the spiced pecans over the salad and serve immediately.

Pairing: Serve with a tangy fruit ale or Octoberfest to offset bitter greens.

SUMMER SALAD WITH BUTTERMILK VINAIGRETTE

1 Rinse and dry the salad greens. Remove and discard all heavy stems. Place the greens in a salad bowl. Peel and pit the peaches, and then chop into bite-sized pieces, and add to the bowl. Add the chopped hazelnuts and crumbled ricotta salata.

2 Whisk together olive oil, vinegar, scallions or chives, parsley, buttermilk, dark honey or molasses, and salt and pepper to taste; whisk until emulsified. Pour over salad greens and toss again.

3 Divide the salad among 4 plates. Garnish with toasted hazelnuts, chive blossoms, if desired.

MAKES 4 SERVINGS

Tip: For a thicker textured salad dressing, blend the buttermilk dressing with the crumbled ricotta salata.

- 2 cups mache or baby lettuce
- 2 cups baby arugula
- 2 large ripe peaches (14 ounces)
- ½ cup toasted chopped hazelnuts
- ½ cup crumbled ricotta salata
- 3 tablespoons extra-virgin olive oil
- 1 tablespoon malt vinegar
- 2 tablespoon minced scallions or chives
- 2 tablespoons minced parsley
- ½ cup buttermilk
- 1 tablespoon dark honey such as buckwheat or molasses
- Salt and freshly ground black pepper, to taste
- Optional garnish: toasted hazelnuts or chive blossoms

Pairing: Harmonize with a peach wheat ale or Belgian pale ale brewed with candi sugar.

ETHIOPIAN CUCUMBER, MANGO & PEPPERS

When Adrienne Pierluissi and Bruno Johnson of Milwaukee's Sugar Maple hosted the OKKA Festival, the Fendika troupe of jazz musicians played two shows back to back. For their break, I catered a spread of Ethiopian food, including homemade injera, a fermented teff flatbread. You can enjoy this salad without the injera; just use butter lettuce as cups for serving.

2 cups seeded and sliced cucumber (1 large cucumber)
2 cups seeded and diced mango, peel removed (2 medium mangoes)
2 tablespoons peanut oil
1 cup diced red bell pepper
1 tablespoon minced red jalapeño pepper (1 small pepper)
1 tablespoon minced green jalapeño pepper (½ small pepper)
¼ cup sliced sweet onion
¼ teaspoon coriander seeds, crushed
¼ teaspoon ground cumin
⅛ teaspoon ground cayenne pepper
⅛ teaspoon powdered cinnamon
1 tablespoon chopped fresh cilantro
3 tablespoons fresh lime juice (juice of one small lime)
3 tablespoons chopped unsalted, dry-roasted peanuts
Salt and freshly ground black pepper, to taste
8 butter lettuce leaves, washed and trimmed

1 Cut the cucumber in half and use the tip of a teaspoon to remove the seeds. Slice the cucumber lengthwise into quarters, and chop into bite-sized pieces. Place in a large glass bowl. Add diced mango.

2 Place peanut oil in a medium skillet (9-inches) and place over medium-high heat. Add bell pepper, jalapeño peppers, onion, coriander, cumin, cayenne, and cinnamon. Cook and stir until onion is just tender. Remove from heat; cool to lukewarm. Scrape the pepper and onion mixture with pan juices into bowl with mango and cucumber.

3 Toss with cilantro, lime juice and chopped peanuts. Add salt and freshly ground black pepper to taste. Serve a mound of salad inside each butter lettuce leaf.

Pairing: A saison or unfiltered Belgian golden ale will heighten spices and aromatics.

SNOW PEA SLAW

The Pennsylvania Horticultural Society created a pop-up beer garden in Philadelphia, with catering by the Jose Garces Group. This is my riff on a recipe served there, using tender snow peas as the base for a crunchy, colorful slaw.

- 2 cups snow peas
- 1 quart boiling salted water
- 2 cups Napa cabbage, cored, halved and slivered
- 1 cup diced daikon radish
- 1½ cups diced celery (about 2)
- 1 cup red cabbage, cored and slivered (about ⅓ of a small red cabbage)
- ½ cup shredded carrots
- Juice of one lemon (about ⅓ cup)
- 1 tablespoon toasted sesame seeds
- ¼ cup slivered candied ginger
- ½ cup Vegenaise or unsweetened coconut cream
- Salt and freshly ground black pepper to taste

1 Blanch snow peas in boiling water for a minute, then drain and cool quickly in a bowl of cold water. Drain in a colander and remove strings and woody tips. Slice the snow peas lengthwise and on a diagonal, into slivers.

2 Mix snow peas, napa cabbage, daikon radish, celery, red cabbage, carrots, and lemon juice in a large bowl. Mix sesame seeds, slivered candied ginger and coconut cream or Vegenaise in a small bowl. Taste and add salt and freshly ground black pepper. Toss the slaw with the dressing and chill for 1 hour before serving.

MAKES 6 TO 8 SERVINGS

IPA BRINED POTATO SALAD

Make this recipe the night before for the best beer flavor. If you're not a fan of hoppy beer, feel free to substitute a mild amber ale and cut the brining time in half.

- **5 pounds redskin potatoes, scrubbed and chopped**
- **1 quart water**
- **1 cup IPA or mild amber ale**
- **½ cup water**
- **½ cup malt vinegar**
- **1 teaspoon celery seed**
- **2 tablespoons brown sugar**
- **1 cup diced onion**
- **1 cup diced celery heart (including some leaves)**
- **¼ cup fresh chopped dill**
- **¼ cup chopped kosher dills**
- **1½ teaspoons smoked or spicy paprika**
- **½ cup Veganaise or sour cream or plain Greek yogurt**
- **6 -8 romaine lettuce leaves (rounded interior leaves) to hold salad**
- **Kosher salt and freshly ground black pepper, to taste**

1 Prepare potatoes by scrubbing and chopping into bite-sized pieces. Bring a quart of water to boil in a large Dutch oven, and add the potatoes. Cook until just tender, about 20 minutes depending on the size and freshness of the potatoes.

2 Meanwhile, bring beer, water and malt vinegar to just below a simmer in a small saucepan set over low heat. There should be wisps of steam but no boiling bubbles. Add celery seed and brown sugar, stirring until sugar dissolves. Remove from heat. Drain the cooked potatoes and place in a 9x13-inch baking dish. Pour hot vinegar and IPA immediately over the hot potatoes, and allow to cool. Stir to coat the potatoes in brine. Cover and chill 8 hours or overnight.

3 After 8 hours or overnight, drain the brined potatoes and place in a large mixing bowl. Mix in chopped onion, celery, dill weed and kosher dill pickles. Mix paprika and Veganaise or sour cream. Toss with potatoes.

4 Wash and trim 6 to 8 romaine lettuce leaves, using the rounded inner leaves. Divide the potato salad evenly among the lettuce leaves, topping evenly. Sprinkle with kosher salt and freshly ground black pepper, if desired. Arrange on a platter and serve.

MAKES 6 TO 8 SERVINGS

Pairing: A brown ale or dunkel will pair with the briny deli flavors of pickles and celery seed in this classic potato salad.

CARAMELIZED GRAPES & GREENS

- 2 cups red grapes
- 1 tablespoon coconut oil
- 2 tablespoons raw honey
- 1 large orange (4 ounces)
- 2 tangerines or clementines (3 to 4 ounces)
- 1 tablespoon fig balsamic vinegar (or aged balsamic vinegar)
- ⅛ teaspoon cayenne pepper
- 1 teaspoon sugar
- 3 cups baby arugula or mesclun lettuce mix (about 4 ounces), washed and dried

Optional: roasted coconut flakes or chopped roasted peanuts

1 Wash the grapes and slice in half. Remove any seeds. Place coconut oil in a large skillet over medium-high heat. Add grapes and honey and stir to coat evenly. Cook until just caramelized. Remove from heat and set aside to cool.

2 Wash the orange and tangerines. Use a zester to collect ½ teaspoon each of orange and tangerine zests; set aside. Over a large quart measuring cup, use a small sharp knife to trim and section the orange and tangerines. First, trim away the peel and white pith on a cutting board. Cut between the membrane and remove fruit and seeds, holding your hands with the fruit over the measuring cup to collect the citrus juices as they drip. You can also do this on a shallow tray with a rim deep enough to collect the juice. Place the segmented citrus in the skillet with the grapes, and stir well.

3 Whisk citrus zests with fig balsamic vinegar, pepper, sugar and ½ cup reserved citrus juices. Stir the zest blend into the skillet with the grapes and segmented citrus fruit. Divide the cleaned greens evenly between 4 plates and top with 2 to 3 large spoonfuls of the fruit mixture, dividing evenly between plates. Garnish, if desired, with roasted coconut flakes and peanuts.

MAKES 4 SERVINGS

Pairing: This is a wonderful fruit salad for winter or early spring. Try with a malty winter beer with substantial raisin character or a bock beer with loads of caramel malt to sweeten the bitterness of the greens.

Boundary Bay Brewery & Bistro BELLINGHAM, WASHINGTON

The Pacific Northwest is legendary for its greenery, gardens and breweries. Little wonder that Lisa Morrison, host of Portland's "Beer O'Clock" radio show and author of "Craft Beers of the Pacific Northwest" praises the Boundary Bay Brewing Co. for its creative menu and award-winning ales such as their flagship IPA and Imperial Oatmeal Stout.

Beyond the fresh beer and food, the Boundary Bay Brewery and Bistro offers a beautiful beer garden that is both respite and reward for customers—and wildflowers, birds and butterflies.

Walk outdoors, and down a flight of steps to reach the terraced beer garden, where shade trees, perennials and native plants thrive nearby picnic tables and benches. Trellises support hop bines, used in dry-hopping specialty brews, planted near an outdoor bar with

taps for fresh draft beer. An open lawn provides audience space for concerts at the music stage, and offers room for kids to run while parents sit and enjoy their beer. It's like a gigantic backyard for beer lovers.

The National Wildlife Federation (NWF) even certified the Boundary Bay Brewery Beer Garden as an official Backyard Wildlife Habitat site. The property attracts a variety of birds, pollinators and other wildlife, while helping to protect the local environment. NWF began the Wildlife Habitat certification program in 1973 and has since certified over 170,000 habitats nationwide. The majority of NWF certified habitats represent the personal commitment of individuals and families to provide refuge for wildlife near their homes, but NWF has also certified more than 4,800 schools and hundreds of business and community sites.

In order to become certified, a property like Boundary Bay's Beer Garden must provide the four basic elements that all wildlife need: food, water, cover and places to raise young; and must employ sustainable gardening practices. Habitat restoration is critical in urban and suburban settings where commercial and residential development encroaches on natural wildlife areas. In addition to providing for wildlife, Boundary Bay Beer Garden conserves natural resources by reducing or eliminating the need for fertilizers, pesticides, and/or irrigation water, which ultimately protects the air, soil and water.

Boundary Bay Brewery is also committed to the Towards Zero Waste campaign. Spent grains from the brewing process go to local farms for livestock and chicken feed and the oil from the Beer Garden fryer is converted to biodiesel by a local vendor. The pub and brewery have completed wastewater and energy audits. Over 70% of Boundary Bay's waste has been diverted from the landfill. The restaurant uses compostable straws and to-go containers, and 100% compostable service ware for outdoor service. Dining tables are made from salvaged flooring.

General manager Janet Lightner says, "We even mark all the items on our menu that include local ingredients with a "Think Local. Buy Fresh" logo so our customers can make informed decisions with their forks and their dollars." From Cascadia Mushrooms to K&M Red River Farms vegetables, Boundary Bay Brewing Co. supports local growers, as well as its own bountiful beer garden. ■

CHAPTER 7

NOODLES & PASTA

CURRIED COUSCOUS WITH ROASTED SHIITAKES

PHOTO: MICHAEL WESSEL

CURRIED COUSCOUS WITH ROASTED SHIITAKES

The fastest-cooking pasta, couscous can be sweet or savory, and in this recipe, elements of both are blended with earthy shiitake mushrooms. Dried mushrooms will work in this recipe as well, just soak in warm water to cover for about 30 minutes before cooking.

- **1** cup couscous
- **3** pitted dates, finely chopped
- **1¼** cups boiling water
- **1** tablespoon coconut oil (or vegetable oil)
- **2** tablespoons minced ginger
- **2** tablespoons minced garlic
- **1** tablespoon ground turmeric
- **½** teaspoon ground coriander
- **¼** teaspoon ground cumin
- **⅛** teaspoon cayenne
- **½** teaspoon black mustard seeds
- **⅓** cup chopped sweet onion
- **⅓** cup chopped red bell pepper
- **⅓** cup chopped celery
- **1** pound shiitake mushrooms, cleaned and sliced
- **1** teaspoon lime juice
- Salt and black pepper, as desired

1 Place couscous and chopped pitted dates in a quart saucepan, and pour 1¼ cups boiling water over; stir to mix. Cover and set aside.

2 While couscous and dates soak, place coconut oil in large skillet over medium heat. Add ginger, garlic, turmeric, coriander, cumin, cayenne and black mustard seeds. Stir and cook until mustard seeds begin to pop. Add onion, red bell pepper and celery and stir. Cover and cook. Trim and slice the mushrooms.

3 Rinse shiitake mushrooms and add to skillet. Stir and cook uncovered, until mushrooms are tender, about 5 minutes. Stir in lime juice. Fluff couscous with a fork, and stir into the curry-mushroom mixture. Heat until juices are absorbed. Season with additional salt and black pepper if desired.

4 Divide evenly among 4 warmed bowls.

MAKES 4 SERVINGS

Pairing: An unfiltered summer wheat ale balances the sweet and spicy flavors and provides creamy carbonation to meld with the fluffy couscous.

BELL'S BEST BROWN ALE AND LEMON PEPPER PAPPARDELLE

PHOTO: JOSHUA SMITH

LEMON PEPPER PAPPARDELLE

Flavored pastas are a pantry staple at home, as just the simplest preparations can be varied with the choice of noodle. Trader Joe's sells a very tasty rendition of lemon-pepper pappardelle.

- 1 tablespoon olive oil
- 3 cloves sliced garlic
- 1 tablespoon minced red chiles or ripe jalapeño
- 8 ounces dried lemon-pepper pappardelle
- 1 cup heirloom tomatoes, seeded, and diced
- 1 tablespoon capers, drained
- ¼ cup extra virgin olive oil
- ¼ cup sliced flat leaf parsley
- ½ cup toasted breadcrumbs or toasted almond slices

1 Bring a large (2 quart) pot of salted water to boil for the pasta. Heat the olive oil in a large skillet over medium heat. When the olive oil is hot, add the garlic and chiles, and turn heat to low.

2 Drop the pasta in the boiling water. Add the tomatoes and capers to the sauté pan, bring to a simmer; stir and cook for 2 minutes.

3 Remove the sauce from the heat and add extra virgin olive oil and parsley. Strain pasta and add directly to the sauce in the skillet. Toss and divide among four serving bowls. Top with breadcrumbs or toasted almond slices.

MAKES 4 SERVINGS

Pairing: Bell's Best Brown Ale makes a harmonious match with the sautéed tomatoes; the slight heat from the jalapeno emphasizes the hoppy finish. Makes a wonderful dish prepared with late-harvest tomatoes.

PHOTO: ROGER BROWN

FUSILLI WITH BASIL-WALNUT PESTO

PHOTO: MICHAEL WESSEL

FUSILLI WITH BASIL-WALNUT PESTO

The Smith House in LA offers more than 120 beers on draft, and always includes several vegetarian options on their menu. Their riff on basil-walnut pesto makes an amazing match with craft beer.

- **8 ounces fusilli or your favorite pasta**
- **⅓ cup chopped walnuts**
- **2 teaspoons minced garlic (or more to taste)**
- **½ cup good-quality extra virgin olive oil, divided**
- **2 cups fresh basil leaves, rinsed and dried, loosely packed**
- **Pinch salt**
- **Pinch red pepper flakes**
- **½ cup freshly-grated Parmesan cheese, divided**

1 Bring a large stockpot filled with one quart water to a boil. Add fusilli and cook according to package instructions.

2 Meanwhile, place walnuts, garlic and 2 tablespoons of the olive oil in a small skillet and cook over low heat until walnuts are slightly golden and garlic is softened and aromatic. Do not let the garlic brown. Scrape the mixture into a food processor fitted with metal cutting blade, or a blender.

3 Add basil leaves, a pinch of salt and red pepper flakes, and ¼ cup oil to the food processor or blender. Cover and pulse on HIGH for a few seconds, then stop, scrape down sides of the container, and blend again. Slowly add remaining oil, pulsing to blend, until pesto reaches the desired consistency. Add 2 tablespoons cheese and pulse on HIGH. Scrape pesto into a large serving bowl, and toss with remaining cheese and hot, drained fusilli.

MAKES 4 SERVINGS

Pairing: Try the Craftsman's Summer Session Ale, or your favorite moderately hopped American golden ale. You can also substitute pistachios for the walnuts, and pair with a more robust Belgian style ale such as Ommegang's Karel.

CREAMY MISO PEANUT NOODLES

PHOTO: MICHAEL WESS

CREAMY MISO PEANUT NOODLES

Do you like celery sticks stuffed with peanut butter? That snack is the inspiration for this crunchy peanut sauce made savory with miso and ginger, tossed with cooked udon, celery and carrots.

1 Bring a large pot filled with one quart water to a boil. Cook soba noodles according to package directions.

2 Meanwhile, place oil, garlic and (if using) fresh ginger into a medium skillet over medium-low heat. Cook until garlic is aromatic, and then stir in peanut butter and citrus juice, stirring until peanut butter is melted. Stir in miso and vinegar, and simmer. Thin with a few spoonfuls of the hot water used to cook the udon. The sauce should be creamy, but not too thick.

3 Add celery to the cooked soba in the pot, and drain immediately. This will blanch the celery to be bright green but still crisp. Place the hot noodles back in the large pot, and stir in the sauce. Stir to coat evenly, and divide between 4 plates. Top noodles with sliced green onions and carrots, and sprinkle with a pinch of cayenne pepper, as desired.

- **1 pound soba noodles**
- **1 tablespoon toasted sesame chili oil or peanut oil**
- **2 cloves garlic, peeled and minced**
- **1 tablespoon fresh grated ginger or 1 teaspoon powdered ginger**
- **3 tablespoons crunchy peanut butter**
- **1 teaspoon lemon or lime juice**
- **2 tablespoons white miso**
- **2 tablespoons rice vinegar**
- **¼ cup hot water from cooking noodles**
- **1 cup sliced celery**
- **½ cup sliced green onions**
- **½ cup shredded carrots**
- **Cayenne pepper to taste**

Pairing: Serve with a spicy ale such as Bad Hare Ginger Beer from Rhinelander Brewing Co. in Wisconsin, or Juju Ginger from Left Hand Brewery. You can also make your own ginger flavored beer by adding a few drops of fresh ginger juice to your favorite pint.

MAKES 4 SERVINGS

UDON WITH GINGER-GARLIC BROTH

PHOTO: MICHAEL WESSEL

UDON WITH GINGER-GARLIC BROTH

For a quick supper, I like to use frozen udon noodles that cook in about the amount of time it takes to boil water. You can find them at Asian markets. Serve with a crisp dry lager, which will pick up the spicy pickled flavors of the ginger.

- 1 pound frozen udon
- 3 cups vegetable broth
- 2 tablespoons roasted garlic
- 2 tablespoons pickled ginger
- 3 tablespoons sliced green onions
- 2 teaspoons toasted sesame seeds, optional

1. Place the fresh udon noodles in large pot and cover with vegetable broth. Place over medium heat.

2. Stir in roasted garlic and pickled ginger and bring to a simmer. Top with sliced green onions and toasted sesame seeds, if desired.

MAKES 4 SERVINGS

Pairing: A black IPA or hoppy American stout can stand up to the garlic-ginger combination.

BEET-RICOTTA GNOCCHI WITH CHEVRE-WEISS SAUCE

Chef AJ Hurst, executive chef of the Vintage Brewing Co.'s pub kitchen, is an adventurous cook, especially in using beer as an ingredient. In this recipe for beet gnocchi, the earthy flavor of the roasted beets are offset by a tangy goat cheese cream sauce, enlivened with the Weiss Blau wheat beer brewed by Scott Manning, Vintage's head brewer. The recipe tastes best when the gnocchi is made with freshly roasted beets, in lieu of canned beets (which will make do as a substitute).

- **3 medium beets (about 3 inches diameter each, total about 1 pound), scrubbed and trimmed; greens may be reserved to cook on the side**
- **1 cup ricotta cheese**
- **½ cup fine grated Parmesan (plus more for sprinkling)**
- **1 whole large egg**
- **2 egg yolks**
- **3 cups all-purpose flour, divided**
- **Salt and freshly ground black pepper, as desired**

1 Prepare the beet puree. Set oven to 400°F, and scrub and trim beets. Wrap beetroots in foil and roast in oven for 2 hours, or until beets are completely tender (pierce easily with a long thin fork). Small beets will cook quickly and require less time.

2 Remove from oven and let cool to lukewarm. Fill a metal bowl with warm water, and unwrap the beets in the water bowl to avoid staining your hands. Rub the beets under water until the skins slide off. Chop the cleaned beets and place in a medium bowl. Mash with potato masher until smooth (you may also use a food processor to puree the beets). Drain off watery beet juice and measure 2 cups purée for recipe. (Leftover beet purée and juice may be added to soups or smoothies.)

3 In a large mixing bowl, blend 2 cups beet puree, ricotta, grated Parmesan, egg and yolks. Season this mixture with ½ teaspoon each salt and pepper. Mix in 2½ cups flour to make a dough. If the dough seems wet, add more flour by the tablespoon. After dough forms a sticky ball, let it rest in a refrigerator uncovered for at least 2 hours. Divide dough into eight pieces. One piece at a time, roll dough out into finger-width ropes (using the extra flour to help prevent sticking). Use a knife or bench knife to cut dough lengths into one-inch pieces. Toss in a bit of flour to seal the edges, and let dough air dry for 30 minutes, uncovered, on a baking sheet in the refrigerator. While dough dries, make the sauce.

BEET-RICOTTA GNOCCHI WITH CHEVRE-WEISS SAUCE CONTINUED

4 Bring a large stockpot filled with 2 quarts water to a boil and add ½ teaspoon salt. Drop gnocchi into boiling and salted water and cook until gnocchi float to surface. Simmer in Weiss sauce until hot and creamy. Sprinkle with Parmesan cheese to finish.

WEISS SAUCE

5 In a large, heavy saucepan over medium heat, sauté the diced onion in butter until it becomes translucent. Add cream and 8 ounces Weiss beer. Reduce mixture by a third, simmering uncovered over low heat, making sure not to boil the cream. After reducing, add the goat cheese in quarters, whisking with each addition, and season with salt & pepper. If sauce seems too thick, thin with a bit more Weiss beer. If desired, add honey to offset bitterness of beer. Place cooked gnocchi in sauce and toss to coat evenly. Garnish with minced fresh tarragon leaves.

WEISS SAUCE

- 2 tablespoons butter
- 1 cup finely diced sweet onion
- 1 cup heavy whipping cream
- 8 -10 ounces Weiss or wheat beer
- 12 ounces goat cheese, at room temperature
- Salt & pepper
- Honey to taste
- 2 teaspoons minced fresh tarragon

MAKES 6 SERVINGS

Pairing: An herbal saison such as Vintage Hibiscus Saison or an Imperial Weiss beer balances the mineral flavors of the beets and creamy cheese sauce.

Brewery Farms

PHOTOS: ROGUE FARMS

Any brewing ingredient that travels to the brewery on the back of a truck or in a shipping container incurs variable costs (but usually higher costs) according to energy prices. So, the closer your sources for brewing ingredients, the better your chances of getting them on time, affordably.

Quality in raw ingredients such as malt and hops vary from year to year, according to temperature, soil conditions, UV intensity, drought, etc. Farm conditions fluctuate across the globe. There's no guarantee regarding crop yields, either.

To deal with all these variables, some breweries are growing their own malt and hops. Many breweries are located in prime agricultural states, and are doing their part to support family farmers. "Farm to foam" breweries include Rogue Ales for its growing its own hops and grain, Sierra Nevada Brewing Co. for its estate ales and Bell's Brewery for its Michigan barley farm.

Since 2009, Rogue has been committed to growing its own ingredients to fuel its beer and spirits lineup. Ingredients produced in Independence, Oregon, include seven varieties of hops, rye, pumpkins (for Rogue's annual Pumpkin Patch Ale), jalapeños (used in Rogue's Chipotle Ale & Chipotle Spirit) and honey from Rogue's own bee hives (Honey Kölsch and 19 Original Colonies Mead).

Rogue also grows two varieties of malting barley at its 242 acre farm in Tygh Valley, Oregon. The barley is floor malted on the farm in the Farmstead Malt House before going to the Rogue Brewery in Newport where it's brewed or mashed to make one of Rogue's ales, porters, lagers, stouts, whiskeys or vodka.

Bell's Brewery plants barley in rotation on an 80-acre farm in Shepherd, Michigan, about a two-hour drive from Kalamazoo. It has been a part of Bell's since 2008. "We grow 2-row barley that is used in Midwestern Pale Ale, Christmas Ale and Harvest Ale," says founder and brewery president, Larry Bell. Once harvested, the barley is then roasted and kilned by Briess Malt & Ingredients Co., Chilton, WI.

The Bell's Farm practices no-till farming to minimize erosion and use of fertilizers, all while improving soil quality. Fields are lined with drain tile to oxygenate the soil and allow earlier planting. All crops are 100% non-GMO (genetically modified organism) with barley sown on different fields over a three-year rotation.

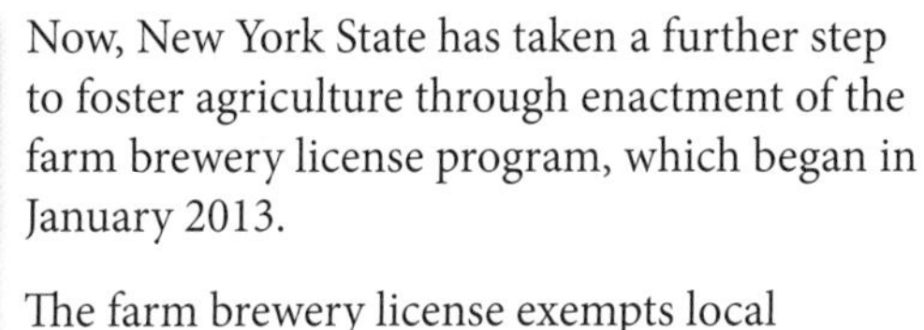

Now, New York State has taken a further step to foster agriculture through enactment of the farm brewery license program, which began in January 2013.

The farm brewery license exempts local breweries from needing additional permits to serve beer and cider by the glass. It also requires breweries to use state-grown

PHOTOS: COURTESY BELLS BREWERY, INC.

HOME BREW CHEF SEAN PAXTON, PHOTO: SETH DOLINSKY, PAUL'S PRODUCE

ingredients, with 20 percent NY-grown ingredients mandated now, and by 2024, fully 90 percent of the beer ingredients must be sourced from NY farmers and growers.

Across the country in California, Home Brew Chef and Slow Food supporter Sean Paxton thinks this is all to the good. "Home brewers who grow their own hops know how fresh, affordable and flavorful their own crops are," he says. "It's also good to recycle spent grain and trub to make compost to improve the soil." He cites the example of Sierra Nevada Brewing Co.'s kitchen garden, which composts organic waste with spent grain, hops and yeast to make new soil to grow the next crops for the restaurant, a full circle.

PHOTO: STONE FARMS

Paxton also works with community supported agriculture (CSA) farms in Sonoma, CA, to source raw ingredients for his cooking and home brewing.

Paxton is inspired by California breweries such as Stone Brewing Co., also supporters of the Slow Food movement, that are committed to sourcing locally grown ingredients. Many ingredients for Stone's restaurant kitchens are grown at Stone Farms, with deliveries coming straight in from the 19-acre fields in Escondido. Their salads and vegetables have the bright flavors and textures of just-picked harvests. The 'farm-to-pint' trend is truly a bounty from breweries. ■

Dinner in the Beer Garden

CHAPTER 8
ROOTS

THAI CARROT BURGERS WITH CUCUMBER RELISH

Pam Percy and Marty Hintz are two talented cookbook authors and also own and run a small farm in Milwaukee County that offers a community supported agriculture (CSA) harvest program. Pam sends out recipes with each week's box of produce, and I especially like this one, adapted to be paired with cucumber relish and a malty lager or Mai bock.

- **2½ tablespoons coconut or vegetable oil, divided**
- **3 ounces (wt) scallions, thinly sliced, including 1 inch of green ends**
- **3 cloves garlic, minced, about 1 heaping tablespoon**
- **1 teaspoon peeled and minced fresh ginger**
- **1 small serrano chile pepper, finely chopped (with seeds if you want spicy burgers)**
- **4 cups grated carrots**
- **1 teaspoon salt**
- **1 teaspoon ground coriander**
- **¾ teaspoon ground turmeric**
- **½ teaspoon ground cinnamon**
- **1 large egg**
- **3 tablespoons peanut butter, melted, cooled to lukewarm**
- **Juice of ½ lime (about 2 tablespoons)**
- **¼ cup chopped cilantro or flat-leaf parsley**
- **1 cup panko bread crumbs**

1 Place a large skillet over medium high heat and add 1 tablespoon oil. When hot, add scallions and cook until they begin to soften, about 1 minute. Add garlic, ginger and chile pepper and stir for 30 seconds, until fragrant. Stir in carrots, salt, coriander, turmeric and cinnamon. Cook and stir 5 to 6 minutes, turning over mixture, until carrots are tender, but not mushy. Set aside until cool enough to handle.

2 In a large mixing bowl, whisk the egg, melted and cooled peanut butter and lime juice. Stir in the carrot mixture and the cilantro. Knead in bread crumbs and let mixture absorb the liquid for about 20 minutes.

3 Preheat oven to 350°F. When cool enough to handle, form the carrot mixture into 4 patties, at least 4 inches in diameter. In an oven-proof skillet placed over medium heat, warm the remaining oil. Brown the patties about 3-4 minutes (use cast iron for best browning). Flip the patties and place skillet in oven to bake 15 to 20 minutes. The patties will be moist and tender, so use a wide spatula with full support to lift and turn the patties. Serve with cucumber relish (recipe follows).

continued

THAI CARROT BURGERS WITH CUCUMBER RELISH CONTINUED

CUCUMBER RELISH

- 1 medium cucumber (6-7 inches long)
- ½ teaspoon sugar
- ¼ teaspoon salt
- 1 small red jalapeno (about 2 inches long)
- 2 tablespoons rice wine vinegar
- 2 tablespoons minced cilantro (or mint)

1 Peel, halve, remove seeds and dice the cucumber, to yield about 1¼ cups. Place in a glass dish and sprinkle with sugar and salt. Halve and remove seeds from red jalapeno, mince very fine, and add to dish. Stir in rice wine vinegar and minced cilantro or mint. Chill until ready to serve. May be made 24 hours in advance, but pepper heat will intensify.

MAKES 4 SERVINGS

Pairing: A malty American lager such as Blue Point Toasted Lager or New Glarus Edel Pils makes a refreshing contrast to the spicy, sweet carrot flavors. You could also try a strong Mai Bock in season, with higher ABV to heighten the jalapeño and ginger.

POTATO-LEEK CAKES WITH ALMOND CREAM SAUCE

PHOTO: MICHAEL WESSEL

POTATO-LEEK CAKES WITH ALMOND CREAM SAUCE

- 2 large russet potatoes (about 1 pound total)
- 2 trimmed medium leeks (about 10 ounces total)
- 2 tablespoons unsalted butter
- 2 tablespoons capers, drained and chopped
- ½ teaspoon freshly ground black pepper
- Nonstick cooking spray
- 1 teaspoon minced garlic
- 2 tablespoons almond oil or vegetable oil
- ½ cup almond butter
- 2 tablespoons fresh orange or tangerine juice
- ¼ teaspoon fresh grated orange or tangerine zest
- ⅛ teaspoon cayenne pepper

1 Peel and cube the potatoes into 1-in. chunks. Place in a large deep saucepan, and cover with cold water (about 2 cups); cover skillet with a tight fitting lid. Bring to a simmer over medium heat.

2 Wash and trim the leeks, slicing in half and, while submerged in a bowl of water, swishing and fanning out the stems to remove all grit. Drain and chop the white base of the leeks and a bit of the green leaves, to yield about 1¼ to 1½ cups. Place in a large skillet with butter, capers and pepper. Sauté leeks over medium heat until tender and golden; remove from heat and set aside to cool to lukewarm.

3 Pierce a potato cube with a fork; when potato falls apart and is completely tender, drain in a colander. Add potatoes to skillet with leek-caper mixture. Mash with a potato masher until combined. When cool enough to handle, wash and oil your hands; form the potato mixture into 4 patties, at least 3-4 inches in diameter.

4 Preheat a griddle over medium-high heat. When hot, coat griddle with nonstick cooking spray and brown the potato-leek cakes on both sides.

5 Meanwhile, prepare almond sauce. Place garlic in small saucepan with almond or vegetable oil. Simmer over low heat 30 seconds, stirring until garlic is just aromatic but not browned; stir in almond butter, orange or tangerine juice and zest, and cayenne pepper. Stir until almond sauce is melted and smooth. Serve potato-leek cakes with almond sauce on the side.

MAKES 4 CAKES

Pairing: A yeasty Belgian strong ale with plum and caramel notes to accent the almonds and golden seared crust of the potato-leek cakes.

SIERRA NEVADA PALE ALE & BEET SLIDERS

PHOTO: JENNIFER MA

BEET SLIDERS

These sliders are inspired by the infamously spicy beet sliders from Gatsby's diner in Sacramento, CA. The original recipe, by chef and co-owners Chuck Caplener and Jared Nuttall, uses 8 arbol chiles for a super-spicy beet. This recipe is moderate in heat, as the hops in Sierra Nevada Pale Ale will accentuate the chiles. To save time, I suggest cooking the whole beets and the avocado spread ahead of time, and sear and assemble the sliders right before serving.

1 tablespoon coriander seeds
1 tablespoon red pepper flakes
1 tablespoon caraway seeds
4 large arbol chiles
1 tablespoon whole black peppercorns
4 large bay leaves
⅓ cup kosher salt
5-6 medium beets, about 3½-4 inches in diameter, scrubbed clean and tops removed
Vegetable oil or nonstick cooking spray

TO ASSEMBLE:

Slider buns (12-16)
2 to 3 tablespoons softened butter
Sweet onion, sliced very thin
Avocado spread (recipe page 130)
Salt and freshly ground black pepper, to taste

1 In a gallon stockpot, combine 2 quarts water and the seasonings. Bring to a boil and add the cleaned, whole beets. The water should cover the beets, so add a bit more as the beets cook. Reduce heat to medium, cover and simmer for about an hour, or until beets are tender.

2 Remove the beets from the stock and let cool until easy to handle. The skins should peel off easily with a vegetable peeler or slide off when immersed in a bowl of cold water. Slice the beets 1/2-inch thick (yields 12-16 slices). If you desire a perfectly round, uniform slice, trim each with a round biscuit cutter, 3 or 4 inches in diameter. Save the trimmings for a beet salad or relish.

3 When ready to assemble, heat a skillet to medium-high heat and add vegetable oil, about 1 teaspoon or use cooking spray to lightly coat the pan. Add the beet slices and sear on both sides until hot and browned, about 2 to 3 minutes per side. While beets cook, toast and butter the slider buns. Stack 1 slice seared beet on a toasted slider bun. Top with thin-shaved sweet onion rings and avocado spread; sprinkle with salt and pepper as desired. Repeat to assemble all sliders and serve immediately.

MAKES 12-16 SLIDERS

BEET SLIDERS CONTINUED

AVOCADO SPREAD

- 2 large ripe avocados, about 10 ounces
- ½ cup sour cream
- ½ cup chopped basil
- ½ cup chopped parsley
- 1 teaspoon grated lemon zest
- 3 tablespoons lemon juice
- Salt and cracked black pepper to taste

4 Combine all ingredients in a food processor fitted with the metal chopping blade; pulse on HIGH until smooth; or mash by hand with a potato masher in a large bowl.

MAKES 2 CUPS

Pairing: The bright hops flavor of Sierra Nevada Pale Ale contrast with the earthy flavor of the red beets, and herbaceous basil in the creamy avocado. A really wonderful pairing.

PHOTO: JENNIFER MARX

KOHLRABI CHIPS

Kohlrabi is one of the lesser known brassica vegetables, with a delicate crispness that makes me think of Asian pears or water chestnuts, and the peppery bite of cabbage. Sliced thin with a mandoline, kohlrabi chips take on the flavor of your favorite marinade. This blend of malt vinegar and smoked salt evokes British chips, good with a mild ale.

1 pound kohlrabi
¼ cup malt vinegar
1 teaspoon smoked salt
¼ teaspoon sugar
Pinch cayenne pepper

1. Wash, peel, and trim ends off the kohlrabi. Place trimmed end down on the cutting board, and cut in half lengthwise, and then slice into crescent wedges about ⅕ inch thick. You may use a mandoline to cut thinner slices, if desired.

2. Toss the sliced kohlrabi with remaining ingredients in a glass dish. Cover and chill 2 hours for best flavor. Makes an excellent snack or side to grilled foods.

Pairing: A brown ale or mild ale will offer sweetness to counteract the bite of the peppery marinade.

MAKES 1½ CUPS

GOOSE ISLAND MATILDA & MANCHEGO POTATO & CHARD TARTS

PHOTO: ROGER BROWN

MANCHEGO POTATO & CHARD TARTS

1 Prepare the cubed potatoes and place in a large Dutch oven or stock pot. Cover with 8 cups water, add 2 teaspoons salt, and bring to a boil. Cook potatoes for 15 minutes, or until tender when pierced with a fork. Drain potatoes in colander and set aside.

2 Place a large skillet over medium heat and add butter, garlic and onion. Stir and cook until onion is translucent, about 5 minutes. Add the sliced chard stems, parsley and jalapeño, and sauté 5 minutes more. Add shredded chard leaves and stir. Cover skillet and remove from heat.

3 Preheat oven to 350°F. Whisk eggs, Cotija cheese and half-and-half together in a large mixing bowl. Add the cooled potatoes and lukewarm onion-chard mixture. Stir well to coat with egg-cheese blend, and divide evenly among the prepared baking dishes. Mix Manchego cheese with smoked paprika and salt, and sprinkle over filled potato mixture. Place baking dishes on a large baking sheet, and place on middle rack in oven. Bake 45 minutes, or until browned.

MAKES 6 SERVINGS

Pairing: The yeasty edge of the Matilda Ale from Goose Island Beer Co. resonates with the baked potatoes gilded with melted Manchego cheese and all its savory, smoky flavors.

- 1½ pounds Yukon Gold or new potatoes, scrubbed and diced into 1-in cubes
- 2 quarts water
- 3 teaspoons salt, divided
- 4 tablespoons butter
- 2 tablespoons minced garlic
- 1 cup yellow onion, peeled and minced
- 8 ounces Rainbow chard, stems cleaned and sliced ¼ inch-thick, leaves sliced into thin shreds
- ¼ cup chopped flat-leaf parsley
- 1 ripe red jalapeño, stem and seeds removed, minced
- 3 large eggs
- 1 cup crumbled Cotija cheese (or ricotta)
- ¼ cup half-and-half
- 3 ounces grated Manchego (or Parmesan)
- ½ teaspoon smoked paprika

- 6 buttered ceramic individual baking dishes, tart pans or cazuelas, about 5 inches diameter

ROASTED BUTTERNUT & BEETS SALAD

PHOTO: JENNIFER MA

ROASTED BUTTERNUT & BEETS SALAD

When you roast a butternut squash, roast another for this salad, as it's so easy to assemble once the squash is cooked. It's a very satisfying salad blend, wonderful with an unfiltered wheat ale.

1 small butternut squash, peeled, seeded, cut into 1-inch cubes (10-12 ounces)
1 tablespoon olive oil
½ teaspoon sea salt
2 small beets, peeled and slivered or shredded into very fine threads (about 1 cup)
1 teaspoon almond or walnut oil
4 cups mesclun mixed greens, washed and stemmed
6 -8 strawberries, hulled and sliced (about ⅔ cup)
3 tablespoons toasted pine nuts, slivered almonds or candied walnuts
2 ounces Romano cheese, shaved
1 tablespoon minced chives

ORANGE JUICE VINAIGRETTE:

⅓ cup almond or walnut oil
⅓ cup orange juice
1 tablespoon minced shallots
1 teaspoon molasses
½ teaspoon grated orange zest
Salt and freshly ground black pepper, to taste

1 Preheat oven to 400°F. Toss cubed butternut squash with olive oil and salt on a baking sheet. Roast until just tender, about 15 minutes. Edges should be caramelized and browned. Remove from oven and let cool.

2 Sprinkle beets with a pinch of salt and toss with almond or walnut oil.

3 Toss mixed greens with cooled butternut squash, beets, sliced strawberries, nuts, and shaved cheese. Whisk together ingredients for orange juice vinaigrette and drizzle over salad. Sprinkle with chives.

MAKES 4 TO 6 SERVINGS

Pairing: Earthy flavors of beets and squash mellow the bitterness of mesclun salad, and pick up the malt notes in the wheat ale. Orange dressing echoes citrusy hops.

SHAVED CELERY ROOT SALAD

This recipe is adapted from one by chef Michel Stroot, one of the most talented chefs working with fresh vegetables. He trained in Europe, where celeriac, aka celery root, is a common staple. Many farm markets offer celery root in the fall, and it's fairly easy to grow in a home garden. The roots are knobby and brown, but the inside flesh tastes like a hybrid of celery, potato and sweet apple.

- **2 to 3 medium celery roots (about 10-11 ounces)**
- **1 tablespoon lemon juice**
- **1 medium tart apple such as Granny Smith or Northern Spy (about 3 ounces)**
- **1 3-inch section daikon radish**
- **1 tablespoon cider vinegar**
- **2 tablespoons almond or vegetable oil**
- **¼ teaspoon sea salt**
- **½ teaspoon freshly ground black pepper**
- **2 teaspoons minced parsley**
- **4 ounces butter lettuce leaves**
- **2 tablespoons toasted almond slices**
- **2 ounces grated Pecorino cheese**

1 Trim, wash and peel the celery roots, and cut into quarters. Using a very sharp knife, or a food processor or mandoline set for thin slices, shave the celery roots into very thin slices. Place in a large glass bowl and sprinkle with lemon juice.

2 Wash, core, and quarter the apple. Cut into very thin slices and toss with the celery root. Peel and slice the daikon radish into very thin slices and toss with the apple and celery root. If the daikon radish is very large, cut the slices into bite-sized halves or quarters.

3 In a small bowl or measuring cup, whisk the cider vinegar, almond or vegetable oil, salt and pepper, and add minced parsley. Toss with the celery root salad.

4 Divide the butter lettuce among four plates. Divide the dressed celery root salad between the four plates, and garnish with toasted almond slices and grated Pecorino cheese.

Pairing: The Full Sail LTD Bohemian Pilsner is pale-golden in color, with a floral hop aroma, malty medium body, and a smooth, thirst-quenching finish. It's ideal with the celery and toasted almond flavors of this salad. You might also enjoy a toasty red Lager or Oktoberfest for a sweet finish.

Building a Better Beer Garden

ADVICE FROM A PRO BREWER

PHOTOS: BELL'S BREWERY, INC.

Have you ever wanted your very own biergarten? Imagine a welcoming social space outdoors, designed with seating where you can relax in the shade, chat and sip beverages in the company of friends and family.

Aaron Rzeznik, a brewer at the Witch's Hat Brewery in South Lyon, Michigan, is also a landscape designer. He studied social garden design while pursuing a degree in landscape architecture. Rzeznik cites several elements of modern beer gardens that can be adapted for homes.

"The Bell's Eccentric Cafe in Kalamazoo, MI, has a contemporary beer garden which emulates the theme from within the building. Inside, the bar appears just as its name implies, 'eccentric,'" says Rzeznik. Random pictures, murals, and memorabilia line the space, giving off an eclectic

AARON RZEZNIK, PICTURED AT GRIFFIN CLAW BREWING CO., BIRMINGHAM, MI

aura. The garden follows the eccentric theme in the elements such as unique chairs and tables, a variety of paving materials and ground cover, wild variety of flora (150 different species), and different spaces for seating, both open and secluded.

Rzeznik also likes the new Griffin Claw beer garden in Birmingham, MI, for its open and social design (pictured). Griffin Claw uses aligning authentic German beer garden style picnic tables which encourage friends, family and strangers alike to interact. Additionally, small movable tables are placed on the far side of the garden allowing for a more intimate experience. A gas fireplace is placed near the center and serves as a gathering place for large groups as well as a source of warmth in the colder months.

Late summer is an ideal time to build a beer garden, as it's possible to get plants, trees and perennials on sale. At the Independent Garden Center Show in Chicago, many growers said that early fall weather is still warm enough to establish plantings, as long as you water and mulch wisely to encourage roots to take hold.

Beyond plantings, elements of a beer garden include an area such as a gravel patio or a floating wooden deck area, where tables and seating can be arranged. Seating can range from traditional folding chairs and benches imported from Bavaria, or simple plank benches built to rest along the edges of square raised beds or wooden planters. A surface to hold food and drinks may be arranged as individual folding tables, or use patio tables to help anchor shade umbrellas.

PHOTO: SIERRA NEVADA BREWING CO.

PHOTO: C.R.PLASTIC PRODUCTS, STRATFORD, ON

Shade is vital, both for people and planters. Traditionally, beer gardens in Bavaria were placed under the deep shade of chestnut trees, their long limbs overhanging caves packed with blocks of ice, where brewers kept their barrels cool all summer long. Modern beer gardens can use pergolas planted with hop vines (or wisteria, as in the case of Sierra Nevada Brewing Co.'s Chico beer garden, pictured above), shade sails, or cantilevered umbrellas over tables to keep everyone cool.

Plantings for a beer garden provide shade, enclosure, color, texture, foliage and flowers. Chestnut trees are traditional, but require a lot of room for roots and canopy. In smaller spaces, a compact Kousa dogwood or serviceberry tree will thrive. Hedge shrubs such as viburnums and arborvitaes or dwarf evergreens can be aligned to completely enclose the space or grouped to form views to draw the eye beyond the garden perimeter.

PHOTOS: LUCY SAUNDERS

Color creates visual accents and improves the overall aesthetics of the space. Colorful planters and built-ins to screen hospitality or utility areas will provide year-round brightness. Plantings with both coarse and fine textures create visual interest.

Lighting the beer garden at night presents little challenge, as there are so many options for solar tiki lights, fire-safe battery-powered votives, and even waterproof electric light fixtures. A firepit or seasonal fireplace can offer warmth well into autumn. Accent lighting in tree branches or under plant leaves will create a soft, unobtrusive glow.

Flowering fragrance is important when planning a beer garden. Mellow, subtle aromas, such as lilac, create a calming background. In contrast, hugely fragrant plants (such as a Bradford pear) can be overwhelming and take away from the appreciation of beer and food. Tropical foliage plants provide seasonal color throughout warm months, without worry about faded blossoms. And training bines of hops on a trellis above an entry gate always makes a welcome symbol for the beer garden. ■

Portions of this profile were published in the *Milwaukee Journal Sentinel,* September 3, 2013

Dinner in the Beer Garden

CHAPTER 9

SQUASH & VEGETABLES

STEVE'S KIMCHI

Thanks to Steve Berthel, a member of the Michigan Brewers Guild, for sharing his recipe, which also makes an amazing broth base for steamed vegetables and tofu.

Allow several days to prepare, and use insulated rubber gloves to hand-mix the kimchi (I could feel the heat of the Korean chilis right through the thin vinyl of standard food-handler kitchen gloves. Just saying…this is spicy.)

- **1 large head Napa cabbage, about 4 to 5 pounds**
- **⅔ cup kosher pickling salt or Korean rock salt**
- **⅓ cup peeled garlic cloves**
- **⅓ cup peeled and sliced fresh ginger**
- **⅓ cup chopped scallions or ramps, cleaned white ends only**
- **¼ cup fresh-squeezed lemon juice**
- **¼ cup fish sauce or kombu infusion**
- **¼ to ½ cup Korean red chili flakes (gochugaru)**
- **2 tablespoons sambal oelek (optional, for extra spicy)**
- **1 cup peeled, chopped daikon radish**

Pairing: Steve recommends, "When kimchi is ready to eat, open slowly in the sink as pressure builds in the jars from the fermentation process. Eat with chopsticks while enjoying a Jolly Pumpkin La Roja."

1 Discard 2-3 outer leaves of cabbage. Quarter the cabbage lengthwise and cut off the woody stem ends. Rinse to remove any grit or debris. Chop cabbage into 2-inch chunks. Spread ⅓ of the cabbage in an even layer in a large glass 9x13x2-inch baking dish. Sprinkle with ⅓ of the salt and repeat layers, using all the cabbage and salt until pan is full (it will be heaping full). Cover pan with a clean chopping board to press the kimchi into the pan. Put a heavy iron skillet or weight on top of the chopping board to press firmly in place. Let cabbage stand 4-5 hours or overnight at room temperature.

2 Place garlic, ginger and scallions into a food processer fitted with the metal chopping blade. Add lemon juice, fish sauce and chili flakes. If you want really hot kimchi, add more chili flakes and some sambal oelek to taste. Pulse food processer on HIGH and grind to a smooth paste. If mixture seems too thick, add a little water, by the spoonful, just enough to get a smooth, spreadable slurry, but not too runny.

continued

STEVE'S KIMCHI CONTINUED

3 When the cabbage is ready, place in a colander and rinse with warm water to remove excess salt. Squeeze liquid out using your hands and place into a large nonreactive (Cambro, glass or porcelain) mixing bowl big enough to hold all the cabbage. Add the chili paste mixture. Wear clean, thick protective gloves (or double vinyl gloves) and knead in chili paste until cabbage is totally mixed. Mix in sliced daikon radish.

4 Pack tightly into 3 sterile pint mason jars, leaving at least 1½ inches of headspace so cabbage doesn't touch the metal lids, loosely seal and let jars sit in a cool, dark space, for 1 to 3 days. Once or twice a day, open jars and use a clean spoon to taste a tiny bit of kimchi; when cabbage is pickled enough to your tastebuds, tightly seal and refrigerate. Keeps 1 to 3 months, as fermentation will continue, but at a much slower pace.

5 To make a sweeter kimchi, add one sliced apple and carrot to the cabbage blend in step 2, or use a mild daikon radish and ripe pear. Some kimchi lovers like to experiment with a mix of orange and lemon juice for the spice paste blend, or use cider or apple juice.

MAKES 3 PINT JARS KIMCHI

Note: This recipe can be adjusted to taste, but the gochugaru chili powder is worth seeking out for traditional flavor—a little sweet and smoky, like paprika, but spicy, too. Unlike dried chili flakes, traditional gochugaru is mostly dried flesh of the chili, with fewer seeds and pith. An American-grown brand of gochugaru can be found at Mother in Law's Kimchi, sold online and at specialty food stores.

BELL'S OBERON ALE WITH AVOCADO & GRILLED CORN SALAD

AVOCADO & GRILLED CORN SALAD WITH ORANGE VINAIGRETTE

- 5 ears corn, husked
- 2 tablespoons olive oil
- 1 cup peeled and diced avocado, sprinkled with lemon juice to prevent browning
- ½ cup toasted pine nuts
- ½ cup scallions, finely sliced
- ½ cup celery, sliced
- ½ cup crumbled feta or ricotta salata
- 1½ cups diced cucumber (ends and seeds removed)

1 Brush corn with olive oil and grill until tender and browned, about 15 minutes. Let cool to lukewarm, then slice off kernels with a short knife, into a large mixing bowl. There should be at least 3 cups kernels.

2 Add diced avocado, toasted pine nuts, onion, celery, crumbled cheese and diced cucumber to the sliced corn. Toss with Orange Vinaigrette, recipe below. Garnish with peeled orange zest, if desired.

ORANGE VINAIGRETTE

- ½ cup olive oil
- ¼ cup fresh orange juice
- ½ teaspoon grated orange zest
- 1 clove garlic
- ½ teaspoon Dijon mustard
- ½ teaspoon salt
- ¼ teaspoon red pepper flakes, or to taste

3 Place all ingredients in a blender, cover and pulse on HIGH until emulsified. Toss with salad and serve immediately. When ready to serve salad, add the dressing and gently toss.

MAKES 6 SERVINGS

Pairing: Bell's Oberon Ale makes a tangy counterpoint to the orange dressing and balances the sweetness of the grilled corn and salty cheese.

RED PEPPERS WITH ORANGE & ROSEMARY

PHOTO: JENNIFER MAR

RED PEPPERS WITH ORANGE & ROSEMARY

The NXNW Brewery in Austin, TX, offered this combination as a special appetizer, and it makes an amazing pairing with amber ale, such as the Duckabush Amber, or Vienna lagers.

5 ripe red bell peppers (about ½ pound per pepper, or 3 lb. total)
1 large sweet orange, halved and fruit sectioned
1 tablespoon capers
1 tablespoon chopped fresh rosemary leaves
½ teaspoon minced garlic
2 tablespoons white balsamic vinegar
2 tablespoons olive oil
Salt and freshly ground black pepper to taste
Toasted baguette slices or 4 to 6 cups mixed greens for plating

1 Prepare a grill for direct cooking over high heat. Use long handled, insulated tongs to hold the peppers about 5 inches from high heat over a charcoal grill or gas flame, turning frequently with tongs until well charred and blackened on all sides. The skins will blister and crack. Place blackened peppers in a brown paper bag and let cool until comfortable to handle, about 15 minutes. Peel off the skin, and remove seeds and stems. Cut the roasted peppers into strips and place in a large bowl. Prepare the orange by cutting in half and scooping out the citrus wedges, discarding peel, pith and white membrane.

2 In an 8-inch skillet, place the capers, rosemary, garlic, peeled orange wedges, vinegar, oil, salt and pepper to taste. Cook over medium-low heat, stirring often, until garlic is fragrant and oranges are juicy. Stir the warmed mixture into the roasted pepper and let it sit at room temperature for 30 minutes for flavors to meld. Serve as a topping for bruschetta or salad with mixed greens.

MAKES 4 TO 6 SERVINGS
(4-5 PEPPER STRIPS PER PERSON)

GRILLED VEGETABLES WITH NEW GLARUS BREWING CO. TWO WOMEN

PHOTO:JENNIFER MAR

GRILLED VEGETABLES

- 1 medium eggplant (about 2 pounds), peeled, ends trimmed and sliced lengthwise
- 1 large zucchini (12 ounces), ends trimmed and sliced lengthwise
- 1 large yellow squash (12 ounces), ends trimmed and sliced lengthwise
- 1 large red bell pepper (8 ounces), sliced and seeded
- 1 cup sliced shiitake mushrooms
- 1 large red onion (8 ounces), peeled, and sliced at least ½-inch thick
- ⅓ cup walnut or vegetable oil
- 2 shallots (2 ounces), peeled and chopped
- 1 teaspoon minced fresh rosemary
- ½ teaspoon minced fresh oregano leaves
- ½ teaspoon dried marjoram
- Juice of one lime (about ¼ cup)
- Salt and freshly ground black pepper to taste
- 1 cup sweet grape tomatoes, sliced in half

MAKES 4 SERVINGS

1 Place prepared eggplant, zucchini, yellow squash, red bell pepper, mushrooms and onion in a large bowl. Blend oil, shallots, rosemary, marjoram, lime juice, salt and pepper in a blender on HIGH until emulsified. Pour over vegetables and toss to coat. Cover and chill one hour.

2 Prepare grill for medium-hot heat. Drain vegetables and reserve marinade. Grill vegetables in a grill basket or grill screen until just tender. When cool enough to handle, chop the cooked vegetables into bite-sized chunks, and place back into bowl with marinade. Add sliced tomatoes and adjust seasoning with salt and pepper. Serve warm or at room temperature.

Pairing: New Glarus Brewing Co. Two Women, is a country lager, deep honey colored with a rich creamy head, medium bodied and malt forward, it is pleasantly reminiscent of a fresh baguette. With the floral aromatics of Hallertau Mittelfrueh, it's a perfect foil for the grilled vegetables.

Note: Deb Carey says, "This is my personal go-to beer. Dan served his brewing Apprenticeship in Bavaria and he has a soft spot for lager beers. He was enamored with Sabine Weyermann's floor malted pilsner malt and was determined to brew a beer for "himself." It was first bottled and sold only at the brewery where he named it Two Women after me and Sabine Weyermann. I could swim in this beer; to me, it tastes just like beer should."

PHOTO:JENNIFER MARX

SUGAR PUMPKIN ON BRAISED MUSTARD GREENS

I first tasted this combination at the Brewers Art in Maryland, as a side dish, but immediately thought that the dish could stand alone. Yes, it's that good. I use warming spices such as ground anise and coriander to heighten the vegetal sweetness of the sugar pumpkin, and season the greens with rice wine vinegar and tamari for a savory edge.

12 ounces mustard greens, cleaned and chopped
1 cup diced sweet onion
2 tablespoons tamari sauce
2 tablespoons rice wine vinegar
1 small sugar pumpkin (also known as pie pumpkin, about 4 pounds)
1 tablespoon vegetable oil
1 teaspoon salt
1 teaspoon ground anise
1 teaspoon ground ginger
1 teaspoon ground cinnamon
¼ teaspoon ground nutmeg
⅛ teaspoon white pepper
2 tablespoons maple sugar or dark brown sugar

1 Heat oven to 375°F. Oil a large roasting dish (at least 9x13x2-inches). Toss the mustard greens with diced onion, tamari and rice wine until well coated. Place in bottom of roasting pan. Add several tablespoons water.

2 Scrub the pumpkin well. Trim a sliver off the base of the pumpkin so it sits flat and steady on the cutting board. Cut quarter wedges away from the sides of the pumpkin. Slice each wedge into pieces about ⅔-inch thick. Trim away any seeds and stringy pith with a small knife. Rub the cut sides of the pumpkin with oil and arrange on top of mustard greens. Mix salt, anise, ginger, cinnamon, nutmeg, white pepper and sugar, sprinkle the spice blend over all. Cover tightly with foil and roast 30 minutes, or until pumpkin is completely tender.

MAKES 6 SERVINGS

Note: Choose a fresh-picked, tender, small pumpkin for this recipe. An older pumpkin with a hard shell will be tough to cut and take twice as long to cook.

Pairing: A yeasty cider, such as Crispin the Saint or North Peak's Nomad, or an unfiltered farmstead ale, to blend with the spice notes in the pumpkin.

PHOTO:JENNIFER MAR

CORN & BEET SALAD WITH WALNUT DRESSING

The Kohler Festival of Beer features a grill-out with more than a dozen top chefs, and this grilled salad is inspired by a relish. It was so crunchy and tasty, I thought it deserved to be enjoyed on its own.

- 4 beets (about 1-1½ lbs), cleaned and trimmed
- 2 tablespoons olive oil
- 4 cloves garlic, divided
- 2 sprigs rosemary
- 2 sprigs fresh sage
- 3 ears corn, or 2 large ears (10 inches)
- 1 small red onion, sliced very thin
- ¼ cup fresh flat-leaf parsley, chopped
- ⅓ cup walnut oil
- Juice of one lemon
- 2 tablespoons malt vinegar
- 1 teaspoon smoked paprika
- 1 teaspoon molasses
- Salt and ground black pepper, to taste
- ¼ cup toasted walnuts
- 6 -8 romaine lettuce leaves, whole

1 To roast beets, prepare the grill (or preheat oven to medium heat, 350°F). Wrap beets in a foil pack with 2 tablespoons olive oil, 2 cloves garlic, rosemary and sage. Roast 1 hour over medium heat. Cool 30 minutes until lukewarm and easy to handle. Peel and chop.

2 Increase grill heat to HIGH. Use long-handled, insulated tongs to place corn over high heat and blacken corn on cobs over a grill or burner. When cool enough to handle, cut corn kernels off the cobs.

3 Mix chopped beets, corn kernels, red onion and parsley in a large glass bowl. In a blender, combine walnut oil with lemon juice, vinegar, remaining garlic, smoked paprika, molasses and salt and pepper to taste. Cover blender and mix on HIGH until emulsified. Toss with beet salad and garnish with toasted walnuts. Serve in romaine lettuce leaves.

MAKES 6 SERVINGS

Pairing: A sour brown ale brewed with cherries or aged in oak barrels gives the tart dimension needed to stand up to smoky-sweet charred corn and earthy roasted beets.

SIERRA NEVADA BREWING CO. TORPEDO ALE WITH ENCHILADAS

PHOTO: JEN

ENCHILADAS WITH MOLE & CHILE-CASHEW CREAM

Perfect for the late summer harvest, this three-page recipe calls for several kinds of chiles—jalapeno, ancho, poblano—in a base of caramelized root vegetables; the sweet heat is accentuated by the hops in Torpedo ale from Sierra Nevada Brewing Co. If a milder enchilada filling is desired, substitute diced carrots or red bell pepper for the poblano chile.

MOLE ENCHILADA SAUCE

2 tablespoons corn oil
½ cup onion, peeled and chopped
5-6 cloves garlic, peeled and chopped
½ teaspoon dried oregano
½ teaspoon ground cumin
⅛ teaspoon ground cinnamon
2 tablespoons ground ancho chili powder
1 tablespoon chipotle chili powder
1 tablespoon paprika
1 tablespoon masa or ⅓ small corn tortilla
6 ounces tomato paste
2½ cups vegetable broth
2 ounces bittersweet dark chocolate, chopped
½ teaspoon salt (optional)

1 Heat oil in a large saucepan over medium-low heat. Add the onion, garlic, oregano, cumin, and cinnamon, stirring to coat with spices. Cover and cook until onion is almost tender (about 5 minutes).

2 Mix in the chili powders, paprika and masa or ⅓ small corn tortilla, blitzed in a blender to crumbs. Stir until mixed in evenly.

3 Gradually mix in the broth and tomato paste, stirring until blended. Increase the heat to medium-high and cook, stirring often, until thickened. Remove from heat; stir in chopped chocolate. Taste and add salt if desired. Set aside for recipe.

continued

ENCHILADAS WITH MOLE & CHILE-CASHEW CREAM CONTINUED

CHILI-CASHEW CREAM

- ½ cup raw cashews
- ½ cup water
- 1 jalapeño pepper, seeded
- ¼ teaspoon salt
- Pinch cayenne

4 Soak cashews in water for at least one hour. Place all the ingredients in a blender or food processor and pulse on the "high" setting until smooth. Reserve for recipe.

continued

Note: This recipe is modeled after a wonderful enchilada served at San Francisco's Gracias Madre, a friendly oasis for vegan food in the Mission District. Thanks to Pete Slosberg for recommending the restaurant!

PHOTO: JENNIFER MARX

ENCHILADAS WITH MOLE & CHILE-CASHEW CREAM CONTINUED

ASSEMBLE ENCHILADAS

- 1 cup peeled and diced sweet potato
- 1 cup washed and diced red skin potato
- ½ cup seeded and diced poblano peppers
- ½ cup seeded and diced red bell peppers
- 1 cup corn kernels
- 1 cup onion, peeled and diced
- 2 tablespoons corn or olive oil
- 1 teaspoon cumin
- ½ teaspoon salt
- ¼ teaspoon freshly ground black pepper
- Jalapeno cashew cream (above)
- Mole enchilada sauce (above)
- 8 8-inch. flour tortillas

5 Preheat the oven to 400°F. Line a baking sheet with parchment paper.

6 Toss the vegetables, onion, oil, cumin, salt, and pepper together in a large bowl. Spread the mixture onto the baking sheet and roast 30-45 minutes or until they are soft and lightly browned, stirring once or twice during the roasting time. Reduce the oven heat to 350°F degrees. Puree in the cooled mole sauce in a blender or use a stick blender to puree smooth.

7 Remove the vegetables from the oven and let them cool a little. Once cooled to lukewarm, slide them off the parchment paper into a large bowl with ½ cup jalapeno cashew cream; toss gently to coat with the cream. Scoop heaping ½ cupful vegetable filling into a tortilla and roll into an enchilada.

8 Pour a little mole sauce into the bottom of a 9x13x2 baking dish. Place each enchilada on top of the mole. Repeat until all enchilada filling is used. Cover the enchiladas with additional mole sauce. If desired, use the remaining cashew cream to drizzle over the mole-covered enchiladas. Bake the enchiladas, uncovered, 20 minutes.

Pairing: Pair with Torpedo from Sierra Nevada Brewing Co., to accentuate the heat of the ancho and poblano chiles.

MAKES 4 SERVINGS
(2 ENCHILADAS PER PERSON)

EGGPLANT WITH SPICY PEANUT-GINGER-LIME SAUCE

You can make this on the grill, or oven roast your eggplant—I like Japanese eggplant for the oven-roasted version as the skin is thin and easy to cook. Add enough hot water to make the sauce creamy and spreadable—which can vary a lot if you use a natural ground nut butter. You may also use some of the nut oil that collects at the top of the jar, instead of the toasted sesame-chili oil.

- **1 tablespoon toasted sesame-chili oil**
- **1 tablespoon minced garlic**
- **½ teaspoon powdered ginger or 2 teaspoons grated fresh ginger root**
- **⅔ cup peanut butter**
- **1 tablespoon tamari sauce**
- **2 teaspoons Sriracha sauce, or to taste**
- **Juice of one lime (about ¼ cup)**
- **⅓ to ½ cup boiling water**
- **2 -3 Japanese eggplants (about 1/2 inches diameter, 10-11 ounces each)**
- **Nonstick cooking spray or 1 tablespoon coconut oil**
- **2 cups shredded napa cabbage or red leaf lettuce**
- **½ teaspoon salt**

MAKES 4 TO 6 SERVINGS

1 Place a medium skillet over low heat and add the toasted sesame-chili oil, garlic and ginger. Cook and stir until garlic is fragrant, about 2 minutes. Stir in peanut butter, tamari, Sriracha, and lime juice. Cook until peanut butter is melted. Whisk in boiling water to thin the blend to desired consistency—the sauce should be thick, not too runny. Remove from heat and set aside.

2 Prepare grill or preheat oven to 375°F. Wash and trim eggplants. Cut in half lengthwise, and then into wedges about 4 inches long, and place on a mesh grill holder or baking sheet. Spray with nonstick cooking spray or brush with melted coconut oil. Grill or roast 15-20 minutes, until tender and edges are browned.

3 Prepare a platter by lining with shredded napa cabbage or lettuce, sprinkled with salt. Arrange cooked eggplant on top, and spoon the spicy peanut-ginger sauce over all.

Pairing: A barrel-aged brown ale, such as the Tyranena Rocky's Revenge, stands up to the savory, spicy sauce but won't overwhelm the tangy flavors of the roasted eggplant.

SESAME MISO-GLAZED SQUASH

A glaze helps soften the hard rind that can develop on yellow squash, harvest in the late summer. This glaze features the mellow saltiness of a brown rice miso – you can also substitute a white miso.

1 Wash and peel yellow squash. Cut into ½-inch thick slices. Place sesame oil in skillet set over medium heat, and brown the sliced squash on both sides. Add miso, orange zest, orange juice and water to the skillet and cover. Steam until the squash is tender.

2 Sprinkle sesame seeds and green onion over the sliced squash. Arrange amaranth leaves (or spinach leaves) on a platter and arrange squash slices on top.

2 medium yellow squash (about 1 pound)
1 tablespoon toasted sesame oil
1 tablespoon brown rice miso
1 teaspoon grated orange zest
⅓ cup fresh-squeezed orange juice
¼ cup water
1 tablespoon toasted sesame seeds
1 tablespoon green onion, minced
Amaranth or spinach leaves

MAKES 4 SERVINGS

Pairing: A malt-forward lager such as Vienna or Oktoberfest balances the salty miso sauce.

PHOTO: MICHAEL WESSEL

CAULIFLOWER-CHICKPEA CAKES

I love falafel, one of the easiest and fastest vegan bar snacks around. Here's a tasty riff on a baked version adapted from Lauren Downey, author of the blog veg-ology. It's a blend of cauliflower and spices folded into a red lentil and chickpea cake. Enjoy with an unfiltered farmstead ale or Belgian-style strong golden ale.

- **1 can (15-16 ounces) chickpeas, drained**
- **½ cup red lentils**
- **4 ounces (wt) chopped cauliflower**
- **2 ounces (wt) chopped carrot**
- **1 cup water**
- **⅓ cup chopped scallions**
- **1 teaspoon minced garlic**
- **¼ cup chopped fresh cilantro or flat-leaf parsley**
- **1 teaspoon cumin**
- **1 teaspoon turmeric**
- **½ teaspoon coriander**
- **⅛ teaspoon cayenne pepper**
- **½ cup panko breadcrumbs**
- **Olive or coconut oil**
- **Salt and freshly ground pepper to taste**

1 Place chickpeas, red lentils, cauliflower and carrot in a large skillet fitted with a lid. Add 1 cup water and turn heat to medium. Cover and simmer over low heat for 15 minutes. Remove from heat and cool to lukewarm. The water should be fully absorbed.

2 Place the lukewarm chickpea-cauliflower mixture in the bowl of a food processor fitted with the metal blade. Add scallions, garlic, cilantro or parsley, cumin, turmeric, coriander, cayenne and breadcrumbs. Cover food processor and pulse on HIGH until mixture forms a thick paste. Or, if you don't have a food processor, mash by hand.

3 Preheat oven to 400°F. Drop ¼ cupfuls of the mixture on a parchment lined baking sheet, and use the back of a spoon or spatula to form cakes, about ½-inch thick, 3-inches diameter. Brush with olive oil or melted coconut oil and add salt and pepper to taste. Bake 15 minutes, remove pan from oven to flip the cakes with a broad spatula, and bake another 5 minutes, or until firm and lightly browned. Serve with diced cucumber-onion relish, recipe follows.

MAKES 4 TO 6 SERVINGS (2-3 CAKES PER PERSON)

CAULIFLOWER-CHICKPEA CAKES CONTINUED

4 Peel cucumber, cut in half and remove seeds. Chop fine, and add minced onion, lemon juice, mint and cilantro. Scrape mixture into a glass dish, stir in tahini and salt, cover and chill. Serve with prepared cauliflower-chickpea cakes.

MAKES 2/3 CUP

CUCUMBER-ONION RELISH

- 4 ounces cucumber
- 2 ounces sweet onion
- 1 teaspoon lemon juice
- 1 teaspoon chopped mint
- 1 teaspoon chopped cilantro
- 1 tablespoon tahini
- Pinch salt

Pairing: Dawney likes a farmhouse ale, Debutante from Brewer's Art, for its refreshing, yeasty character to balance the seasonings and earthy lentils. I also like an English bitter, which is malty and bracing, for a refreshing finish.

PHOTO: MICHAEL WESSEL

HEIRLOOM TOMATO SALAD

Yes, tomatoes are fruits, although they are sold as vegetables, and many people associate their flavors with savory cooking. Heirloom tomatoes are often more delicate than most commercially grown varieties, so try to find them at a farmer's market, or better yet, grow your own. Add fresh herbs as you like – chive, marjoram or basil are good. Make large croutons as a garnish.

1 Place the sliced tomatoes on a large platter. Arrange overlapping circles of the cucumber slices and top with cured olives. Drizzle with extra virgin olive oil and the juice of one half lemon. Sprinkle with salt and freshly ground black pepper. Garnish with herbs, and croutons if desired.

3 heirloom tomatoes (about 1½ pounds total)

1 cup cucumber slices

1 cup assorted cured olives

2 tablespoons extra virgin olive oil

One half lemon

Coarse sea salt and freshly ground black pepper

1 to 2 tablespoons chopped fresh herbs such as chive, marjoram or basil

Toasted croutons, optional garnish

Note: The River City Brewing Co. of Sacramento, CA, served an Heirloom Tomato Sorbet with its Kölsch at a recent Farm to Fork beer and food dinner. To make a sorbet, chop 3-4 large heirloom tomatoes, removing seeds and woody cores. Puree in a blender with ½ cup tomato juice, ¼ cup sugar, 1 tablespoon lime juice and a pinch salt. Push through a large mesh sieve. Freeze in an ice cream maker according to manufacturers' directions. Serve with a savory shortbread or millet flatbread, page 178. Or serve tiny scoops on top of thick slices of cucumber, each garnished with a ripe olive.

Pairing: Enjoy with a bready Continental Pilsner or Kölsch, to highlight the sweetness of the tomatoes without battling the herb flavors.

ZUCCHI ROLL

PHOTO: LIBBY VANDE

ZUCCHI ROLL

My friend Libby VanderPloeg designed the WELL SEASONED cookbook, and contributed the recipe and photo for these creative zucchini rolls.

- **1 sweet potato, peeled and cut into 1-inch dice**
- **1 teaspoon olive oil**
- **1 teaspoon salt**
- **1 teaspoon chili powder**
- **¼ teaspoon ground white pepper**
- **2 large zucchini, washed and ends trimmed, sliced lengthwise into ⅛-inch thick ribbons**
- **1 cup chopped fresh arugula**
- **1 cup chopped fresh cilantro**
- **10 cherry or grape tomatoes, halved**

1 Boil the diced sweet potato with 1 cup water in a large skillet over medium-high heat, until tender. Drain and transfer to a food processor fitted with the metal chopping blade. Add olive oil, salt, chili powder and white pepper, and blend until smooth.

2 Steam the zucchini strips in ½ cup water in a large skillet, covered, for 5 minutes, or until flexible. Remove strips and arrange on a clean cutting board.

3 When zucchini strips are cool enough to handle, assemble rolls by spreading the sweet potato mixture across each strip; sprinkle with chopped arugula and cilantro. Roll up each strip gently, so filling stays in place. Secure each roll with a toothpick as shown, and garnish with a halved piece of cherry tomato. Serve immediately.

MAKES 15-20 ROLLS

Pairing: A spicy unfiltered Belgian-style golden ale brewed with orange zest and coriander enhances the flavor of the squash.

Beer gardens along Virginia's Brew Ridge Trail

PHOTO: BLUE MOUNTAIN BREWERY

PHOTO: NELSONC

Gorgeous beer gardens (and equally beautiful beer) can be found across the Blue Ridge Mountains in Virginia, all along on the Brew Ridge Trail.

Start the trek in Charlottesville, within walking distance of the downtown pedestrian mall. Stay at the Omni Charlottesville, and enjoy an enormous breakfast buffet, replete with cheddar grits and sage biscuits. Another breakfast option can be found at Beer Run, one of Charlottesville's top craft beer retailers. The kitchen serves breakfast wraps, paninis and omelettes to get you primed for a day of travel and tasting.

Nelson County's craft beer breweries may be tucked in the foothills, but steep demand means expanding beer gardens. Blue Mountain Brewery, located in Afton on Route 151, just opened its new kitchen, plus a large beer garden overlooking the mountains. The expansion almost doubles the dining room, and the former pub area has been converted into The Blue Mountain Beer Hall. "We're gaining quite a bit of space for our thirsty customers," says Mandi Smack, co-owner of Blue Mountain.

The Devils Backbone Brewpub, also called the Basecamp, is located in Rosedale, VA, at the base of the ski mountain for the Wintergreen Resort. The resort is a convenient and luxurious place to stay with rental condos and suites, as well as a plush spa, tennis and ski lessons in season.

Devils Backbone Basecamp is housed in a charmingly rustic lodge, modern yet woodsy, with a huge bar, beer garden with deck and restaurant. Their nearby production brewery, the Devils Backbone Outpost, offers a tasting room and beer garden. According to brew master Jason Oliver, the Basecamp Brewpub serves as a pilot brewery. Oliver has led Devils Backbone to 7 gold medals and 16 additional medals at the Great American Beer Festival™ and was named Small Brewing Company and Small Brewing Company Brewer of the Year in 2013.

PHOTOS: DEVILS BACKBONE BREWERY

In nearby Nellysford, Wild Wolf Brewing Co., a brewery, restaurant and homebrew supply shop, is run by Mary Wolf and her son Danny, who started the brewery in a former school house. The dog-friendly beer garden with gazebo is shaded by old elm trees, within earshot of a working water wheel and framed by rustic views.

"We have expanded our beer garden significantly since we opened two years ago," says Wolf. "The sheer raw beauty of the area, combined with enjoying our beer and food outdoors, creates an irresistible combination!"

The Brew Ridge Trail celebrates the craft beer industry in Nelson and Albemarle Counties. The six breweries that comprise the trail offer award-winning beer in unique settings, with updates posted on www.brewridgetrail.com. ■

PHOTOS: WILD WOLF BREWING CO.

CHAPTER 10

GRAINS

CARROT RISOTTO CAKES WITH SPICED PLUM RELISH

PHTO: JENNIFER MARX

CARROT RISOTTO CAKES WITH SPICED PLUM RELISH

Adapted from a carrot risotto enjoyed with an Allagash White ale at a beer dinner in Denver, these carrot risotto cakes make the most of the rice's sticky texture, while the spicy plum relish highlights the carrot's sweetness.

- 3 cups vegetable broth
- 1 cup water
- 1½ tablespoons butter, divided, softened
- 1 cup minced Vidalia onion
- 2 tablespoons minced garlic
- 2 cups finely grated carrot (about 4 medium)
- Coarse salt and ground pepper
- 1¼ cups Arborio or short-grain rice (do not substitute long/medium-grain rice)
- ⅓ plus ¼ cups grated Asiago cheese, divided
- 2 cups panko breadcrumbs, divided
- 3 large eggs, plus 1 egg white
- ¼ cup chopped parsley leaves
- 2 tablespoons chopped thyme
- 1 teaspoon grated lemon zest
- Canola oil (for frying)
- Arugula or mesclun salad mix

1 In a large saucepan, heat broth and water over medium heat until simmering. In a separate 2-quart saucepan, melt 1 tablespoon butter over medium heat. Add onion, garlic, and carrots; season with salt and pepper as desired. Cook, stirring occasionally, until caramelized, 10 to 12 minutes. Stir in rice. Add ½ cup hot broth; cook, stirring, until absorbed, 1 to 2 minutes. Add 2 cups hot broth; simmer over medium-low, stirring frequently, until mostly absorbed, 10 to 12 minutes. Continue to add broth, about a cup at a time, stirring and cooking until absorbed before adding more. Cook until rice is thick, creamy and tender, about 20 minutes (you may not need all the broth).

2 Remove risotto from heat. Stir in ⅓ cup grated Asiago cheese. Let cool. Stir in ½ cup panko breadcrumbs, 1 beaten egg, parsley, thyme and lemon zest. Chill 2 hours. Grease your hands with butter and scoop and press risotto into 8-10 cakes, about 3 inches in diameter. Arrange on a baking sheet lined with parchment paper and chill until firm (overnight is fine). Meanwhile, prepare the Spiced Plum Relish (recipe below).

continued

CARROT RISOTTO CAKES WITH SPICED PLUM RELISH CONTINUED

Pairing: A peppery Imperial Weizen ale supports the spicy plum relish, and offers creamy effervescence to meld with the tender risotto cakes. A strong ale brewed with ginger root or a spiced hard cider would be refreshing.

3 To make the cakes, preheat oven to 250°F. Set a parchment-lined baking sheet in oven. Beat 2 eggs and 1 egg white in shallow bowl to blend. Place remaining panko breadcrumbs in another shallow bowl. Pour enough canola oil into large skillet to coat bottom; heat oil over medium-high heat. Put a risotto cake on a wide fork or slotted spatula, and dip into beaten egg, then into panko crumbs to coat. Use fork to slide cake into hot oil. Working in batches, sauté risotto cakes in hot oil until crisp and brown, about 2 to 3 minutes on each side. Transfer cooked cakes to baking sheet in oven.

4 Serve risotto cakes dusted with remaining grated Asiago cheese, on top of arugula or mesclun lettuce mix, garnished with Spiced Plum Relish.

SPICED PLUM RELISH

- 3 ripe plums, unpeeled, pitted and finely diced, (1½ cups)
- ¼ cup rice vinegar
- 1 tablespoon minced fresh ginger
- 1 teaspoon grated orange zest
- Pinch powdered allspice
- ⅓ cup sugar
- Pinch salt, optional
- Pinch cayenne, optional

SPICED PLUM RELISH

5 Place all relish ingredients in a nonreactive stainless 1-quart saucepan. Simmer over medium heat until thickened, stirring often. Remove from heat; taste and adjust seasonings as desired. Add cayenne if the heat from the ginger is not enough for your palate.

MAKES 1½ CUPS

KASHA WITH BEETS & SOUR CHERRIES

This is a riff on a favorite recipe from Veselka, the classic NYC Village diner featuring eastern European foods. The addition of dried sour cherries enlivens the kasha, and harmonizes with the dark malts in a black beer.

1 Cook kasha according to package directions, to yield 2 cups. Mix kasha, beets and sour cherries. In a blender, puree the orange zest, onion, parsley, olive oil and raspberry vinegar. Pour dressing over over the kasha and toss well to coat evenly. Serve with red lettuce leaves.

MAKES 4 SERVINGS

- **2 cups cooked kasha**
- **1 cup diced cooked or pickled beets**
- **½ cup dried sour cherries**
- **1 teaspoon grated orange zest**
- **¼ cup minced red onion**
- **¼ cup chopped parsley**
- **¼ cup olive oil**
- **¼ cup raspberry vinegar**
- **4 red lettuce leaves**

Pairing:
Black lager or barrel-aged brown ale

RED QUINOA SALAD WITH AVOCADO CREAM

PHOTO: MICHAEL WESSE

RED QUINOA SALAD WITH AVOCADO CREAM

This is a perfect dinner salad for September, when tomatoes are at their peak. Mad Fox Brewing Co. of Falls Church, VA, served a slightly different red quinoa salad at its annual vegetarian beer dinner in 2012, with Guajillo pepper salsa instead of plain sliced tomatoes.

1 Prepare quinoa according to package directions. Typically, one cup dry quinoa yields 3 cups cooked. While quinoa cooks, prepare and combine basil, spinach, tomatoes, onions, celery and olives. Let quinoa cool to room temperature and fold into salad mixture. Divide among 6 plates and top with several tablespoons of spicy avocado cream, recipe below.

- 3 cups cooked red quinoa
- 2 cups chopped basil
- 2 cups chopped baby spinach or arugula
- 12 cherry tomatoes, quartered
- 2 yellow tomatoes, quartered
- 3 green onions, sliced
- ½ cup chopped celery
- 1 small can (2.25 ounces) sliced olives, drained

MAKES 6 SERVINGS

AVOCADO CREAM

2 Place all ingredients in a blender and pulse on HIGH until smooth. If mixture seems very thick, you may add a bit more buttermilk and blend again. Cover and chill until ready to serve.

AVOCADO CREAM

- 1 cup coarsely mashed very ripe avocado
- 2 tablespoons lime juice
- ⅓ to ½ cup low-fat buttermilk
- 2 tablespoons chopped parsley
- 1 tablespoon chopped celery leaves
- ¼ teaspoon smoked chipotle chili powder, or to taste
- ½ teaspoon salt
- ¼ teaspoon freshly ground black pepper
- ¼ teaspoon cayenne pepper
- ½ to 1 clove garlic, peeled and crushed

Pairing: A robust Oktoberfest or Marzen lager with lots of caramel malt melds with the nutty flavors of the red quinoa, and is strong enough to match the spicy flavors in the chili-spiked avocado cream.

PILSNER CORNBREAD WITH CHILE CREAM

PHOTO: MICHAEL WESSEL

PILSNER CORNBREAD WITH CHILE CREAM

- 1 cup pilsner, plus more if needed
- 1 cup medium-grind cornmeal (I use Bob's Red Mill)
- ½ teaspoon salt
- 1 cup self-rising flour
- 3 tablespoons dried buttermilk powder
- 3 tablespoons sugar
- 1 large egg
- 2 tablespoon cream
- 2 tablespoons melted butter
- Cashew chile cream, see page 156
- Roasted red pepper strips

1 Preheat oven to 375°F. Mix lager and cornmeal in a glass dish, cover with plastic wrap, microwave on high heat for one minute, and set aside to cool (cornmeal will absorb the beer). Sift salt, flour, powdered buttermilk and sugar.

2 Whisk together the egg and cooled cornmeal, add cream and melted butter and mix again. Stir into the sifted dry ingredients until just blended (do not overmix, or bread will be tough). If the batter seems too stiff, stir in another tablespoon or two of the pilsner.

3 Grease a 8x8x2-inch baking pan liberally with butter. Pour batter into the pan, and place pan on middle rack of preheated oven. Bake 25 minutes, or until cornbread is browned and cooked through. To test, insert a wooden toothpick in center of cornbread—when it comes out clean, it is done. Remove from oven and let cool. Brush with cashew chile cream and top with several strips roasted red peppers.

YIELDS 6 PIECES

Pairing: A light Kölsch or American pilsner will make a cooling match with the chile cream and roasted peppers.

Note: The beer is baked into the batter for this tender pilsner cornbread—and if you prefer real cheese, may I suggest Martha's Mighty Fine Food's Pimento Cheese as an alternative topping? This gold-medal-winning cheese spread from Milwaukee is a readymade version of the Southern classic blend of grated Cheddar and minced roasted red pimento peppers. Find it online at larrysmarket.com.

MILLET FLATBREAD WITH MANCHEGO AND ROSEMARY

One of the early adopters of Chicago's craft beer scene was Jerome's restaurant on Clark Street, serving more than just macro brews in the mid-1980s. Their crunchy millet bread was featured in GOURMET magazine—I tweaked the recipe into a flatbread, topped with slivered olives, grated Manchego and minced rosemary.

- 2 tablespoons honey
- 1 package active dry yeast
- 1 cup warm water (105°F to 115°F degrees)
- 1 tablespoon olive oil
- 1½ cups whole wheat flour
- 1 teaspoon salt
- ¾ cup whole millet
- 1½ cup to 2 cups all-purpose flour, as needed
- ⅓ cup slivered oil-cured olives
- ½ cup grated Manchego cheese
- 1 tablespoon minced rosemary

Pairing: These crunchy flatbreads are wonderful with a golden ale aged in merlot barrels, or a farmstead dry cider with enough tannins to take on the Manchego and rosemary.

1. Mix honey and yeast in warm water in large bowl; let stand 5 minutes, or until bubbly. Stir in oil, 1 cup whole wheat flour and salt. Let rise, covered, in a warm place 1 hour, or until doubled.

2. Stir in remaining whole wheat flour and millet. Stir in all-purpose flour, ½ cup at a time, until dough forms a ball and pulls away from sides of bowl. Knead dough on lightly floured surface until dough is smooth and elastic. Put dough into a large oiled mixing bowl; turn dough ball over to oil on all sides; cover with a damp tea towel. Let rise in warm place until doubled, about 1 hour.

3. Punch down dough; cut in sixths. Shape each piece into round flatbread. Put rounds onto parchment-lined baking sheets; cover with damp tea towels and let rest 20 to 30 minutes.

4. Heat oven to 350°F. Top the flatbreads with olives, cheese and rosemary, dividing evenly among the six flatbreads. Bake until browned on edges, about 20-25 minutes. Remove from oven and let cool to lukewarm. Serve immediately.

MAKES 6 SERVINGS

RISI E BISI WITH CORIANDER-SPICED SHALLOTS

I make these with Arborio or Asian sushi rice, and form into small bite-sized balls —they are pretty and tasty, topped with the coriander-spiced shallots and paprika.

- 6 cups water or vegetable stock
- 1½ cups arborio or sushi rice
- 1 garlic clove, minced
- 1½ cups fresh peas
- 2 tablespoons extra virgin olive oil
- 1½ cups slivered shallots or sweet onion
- 1 teaspoon ground coriander
- ¼ teaspoon ground white pepper
- ½ teaspoon paprika
- ½ teaspoon salt

1 Pour stock or broth into a large saucepan fitted with a lid, and bring to a simmer. Add Arborio or sushi rice and garlic. Cover and simmer until rice has absorbed almost all the water. Stir in the peas. Cook 3-4 minutes, or until peas are bright green and tender. Remove from heat and let cool to lukewarm.

2 While rice cools, place a small skillet over medium heat and add olive oil and shallots or onion. Cook and stir until shallots are well coated with oil. Season with coriander, white pepper, paprika and salt, and cook until completely tender. Taste and add more seasonings, if desired. Remove from heat and let cool to lukewarm.

3 Use a 1-oz. scoop or large tablespoon to pick up warm rice-pea mixture and form into balls. Lightly oil or butter your clean hands to form the rice balls without sticking. Place on a serving dish. Top with a pinch of cooked shallots. Continue until all the rice balls are formed.

MAKES 4 TO 6 SERVINGS (2-3 PIECES PER PERSON)

Pairing: These make a terrific match with a spicy pumpkin ale such as Ichabod from New Holland Brewing Co. or an autumn ale such as the Tumbler Brown Ale from Sierra Nevada Brewing Co.

PHOTOL MICHAEL WESSEL

Botanical Garden Brewfests

More than a dozen public gardens across America now offer beer festivals as part of their annual events. One of the largest is the Fest-of-Ale at the Missouri Botanical Garden, now in its sixth year. Each October, the large pool and fountain in the middle of the courtyard are lined with booths filled with avid beer fans.

PHOTO: MISSOURI BOTANICAL GARDEN

With 20 breweries and the Square One distillery attending, it was a full evening of tasting and food sampling. Many breweries created fall beers with nuts, pumpkin and herbs, such as Ferguson Brewing's Pecan Brown Ale and a pumpkin ale. Ferguson is based near a local farmers' market, and the brewery's spent grain is very popular for compost with the farmers there. In turn the brewery gets botanicals for their beer from the local farmers who get their grain, a wonderful full circle.

Piney River Brewing Co.'s Black Walnut Wheat Ale was delightful, brewed with black walnuts from Hammon Nuts, one of the few remaining suppliers for wild sourced nuts. In addition to the tasting, a local home brew club, the St. Louis Brews, conducted demos about home brewing.

PHOTO: THE OREGON GARDEN

In Georgia, the Atlanta Botanical Garden hosts a weekly beer tasting through the month of October, to celebrate the harvest season with a selection of seasonal brews and live music. Fest-of-Ale includes art classes, a pumpkin carving contest, and fall-themed ales such as Blue Point Pumpkin Ale, Bridgeport Witch Hunt, Red Brick Hoplanta, and RJ Rockers Son of a Peach.

At the third annual Chicago Botanic Garden festival, "Autumn Brews: Seasonal Beer Tasting in the Garden," the gardens are open in the evening. Guests can sample and stroll among the harvest displays and fall seasonal plantings. With a strong list of local breweries, including Argus, Baderbrau Brewing Co., Bell's Brewery, Inc., Berghoff Brewery, Finch's Beer Co., Emmett's Brewing Co., Four Horseman Brewing Co., Lake Bluff Brewing Co., Lagunitas Brewing Company and Sprecher Brewery, the fest is relaxed and low-key.

Held in spring, the Oregon Garden Brewfest takes place under twinkly white lights in the Frank J. Schmidt Pavilion on the grounds of the Oregon Garden in Silverton, OR. Attendees stroll through the lush landscaping of the Oregon Garden

PHOTOS: THE OREGON GARDEN

PHOTOS: ATLANTA BOTANICAL GARDEN

as they sample beers from more than 60 breweries. Crowds squeezed together to enjoy music by regional bands, or study up on beer tasting in educational sessions with Ginger Johnson, owner of Women Enjoying Beer.

Many attendees played it smart and booked rooms at The Oregon Garden Resort, right up the hill from the festival. The festival spans three days and draws more than 8,500 beer lovers. Oregon is known for its craft beers and ciders, but most of the big festivals celebrating them are held in Portland, Eugene and Bend. It's wonderful to have a beer festival in the central Willamette Valley and introduce beer fans to the beauty of the Oregon Garden.

And given how many botanical gardens offer wine tastings to their patrons, it would be inspiring to see even more garden programs embrace the craft beer community. ■

Dinner in the Beer Garden

CHAPTER 11
SAUCES & SOUPS

WISCONSIN BEER & CHEESE SOUP

PHOTO: MICHAEL WESSE

WISCONSIN BEER & CHEESE SOUP

Recipe tester Rebecca Wright says, "My husband doesn't like most cheese soups, but loved this." It's an easy recipe to make ahead, but be sure to warm gently over very low heat, as the cheese can scorch.

- 1 cup finely diced carrots
- 1 cup finely diced onion
- 1 cup finely diced celery
- ⅓ cup butter
- 5 garlic cloves, peeled and minced
- ½ cup all-purpose flour
- 2 cups vegetable broth
- 12 ounces red ale or bock, at room temperature
- 1 teaspoon hot sauce, or to taste
- salt and black pepper, to taste
- 1 teaspoon Dijon mustard
- 1 teaspoon dry mustard
- 1 teaspoon Worcestershire sauce
- 1 cup cream
- 2 cups half-and-half
- ½ cup crumbled Gorgonzola, room temperature
- 8 ounces cream cheese, room temperature, cut into 1-inch cubes
- 4 cups shredded sharp Cheddar, room temperature
- Garnish: diced red bell pepper, minced scallions (green onions), or popcorn

1 In a one gallon stockpot, simmer carrots, onions, and celery in butter for 10 minutes. Add garlic, cook additional minute. Add flour, a bit at a time and stir constantly. Cook roux for a few minutes. Stir in broth, beer, mustards, Worcestershire sauce, hot sauce, salt and pepper. Bring to a simmer and heat 10 minutes.

2 Turn heat to low and whisk in cream, half and half and Gorgonzola, stirring until melted, then add cream cheese one cube at a time, whisking until smooth after each addition. Remove from heat, and whisk in grated Cheddar cheese, ¼ cupful at a time, stirring constantly. You can make the soup base the night before, reheat to simmer, and add grated Cheddar cheese just before serving.

MAKES 2½ QUARTS

Pairing: An Irish red ale will heighten the sweet dairy flavors of the cheese, while a smoked porter will bring up the savory pepper flavors.

PARSNIP & WHITE CHOCOLATE CREME

This is delicious hot or cold, and makes a fantastic starter for a Valentine's Day chocolate dinner.

- **2 pounds parsnips (5 large parsnips)**
- **1 cup vegetable or caramelized onion stock, plus 2 quarts**
- **3 tablespoons butter**
- **1 cup white onion, peeled and chopped**
- **2 cloves garlic, peeled and chopped**
- **Salt, to taste**
- **½ teaspoon white pepper, or to taste**
- **1 teaspoon vanilla extract**
- **4 ounces white chocolate, chopped**
- **1 cup heavy cream**
- **Garnish: Meyer lemon wedges**

Pairing: Pair with moderately bitter ale or dunkelweizen, to offset the sweetness of the chocolate and root vegetables.

1 Preheat oven to 375°F. Peel parsnips, and cut in large chunks and place in 9x13x2 roasting dish. Cover with 1 cup stock and cover dish with foil, crimping edges to seal. Cook 1 hour or until completely tender.

2 Melt the butter over medium-low heat in a large stockpot fitted with a lid, and gently sauté the onion and garlic until translucent, about 1 minute. Add remaining stock and parsnips. Season with salt and white pepper, cover and simmer until the parsnips are falling apart, about 20 minutes.

3 Remove from heat and stir in vanilla extract, white chocolate and heavy cream. Using an immersion or stick blender, pureé until smooth. Taste and adjust seasonings, and serve garnished with wedge of Meyer lemon.

MAKES 2½ QUARTS

MUSHROOM COCOA STOUT SAUCE

FreshCraft is one of Denver's top destinations for craft beer and food, with a good selection of vegetarian dishes such as tacos stuffed with cocoa-dusted chiles and cremini mushrooms. The flavors inspired me to blend them in a stout-infused sauce, to top grilled chiles and plantains.

- 1 tablespoon olive oil
- 1 cup chopped yellow onion
- 1½ tablespoons minced shallots
- 8 ounces (wt) cremini mushrooms, thinly sliced
- 2 tablespoons minced fresh jalapenos
- 2 tablespoons tomato paste
- 2 tablespoons cocoa powder
- 6 ounces (fl) sweet stout
- 1 cup vegetable broth
- Freshly ground black pepper, to taste
- ½ teaspoon ground chipotle
- 1 teaspoon smoked paprika
- 1 teaspoon lime juice
- 1 ounce (wt) bittersweet chocolate, grated
- Sea salt, to taste
- 1 pound fresh pasilla chiles, roasted, cleaned and seeded
- 8 ounces grilled plantain, sliced
- ⅓ cup toasted pepitas, to garnish

1 Place olive oil, onion, and shallots in a large skillet over medium heat; cook and stir until soft and translucent. Add mushrooms and jalapenos; cook until mushrooms are softened. Add tomato paste and stir well.

2 Whisk cocoa powder into the stout until smooth. Add to skillet with vegetable broth, pepper, chipotle, paprika and lime juice. Stir well. Bring to a simmer and reduce heat to low; simmer 15 minutes.

3 Remove 1½ cups or several ladles of the sauce mixture and place in blender. Cover and use a folded towel to hold blender lid in place while pulsing on HIGH. Blend until smooth, and whisk the creamy emulsion back into the skillet mixture. Remove from heat. Stir in grated chocolate, and add salt as desired. Serve over grilled chiles and plantains, with toasted pepitas if desired.

MAKES 4 SERVINGS (3 CUPS SAUCE)

Pairing: Sweet stout to echo cocoa, or bock lager to cut richness of sauce

CARAMELIZED ONION PHO

For best flavor, make the broth a day ahead of time.

- 6 pounds sweet onions, peeled and chopped
- 2 tablespoons minced garlic
- 3 tablespoons toasted sesame oil
- 1 pound leeks (1½ large), white and tender green parts, sliced, washed and chopped
- 2½ quarts water
- 2 stalks lemon grass, chopped
- 4 star anise pods
- 3 -inch fresh ginger root, peeled and chopped
- 1 tablespoon black peppercorns
- 3 -inch cinnamon stick, broken
- 2 tablespoons white miso, plus more as needed
- ½ pound fine rice stick noodles
- 4 ounces (wt) carrots, peeled and julienned
- ½ cup Thai or purple basil leaves
- ⅓ cup chopped scallions
- 1½ cups mung bean sprouts
- 2 tablespoons jalapeno chiles, minced or ¼ teaspoon cayenne
- 6 lime wedges
- ⅓ cup chopped cilantro, optional garnish
- ¼ cup chopped mint leaves, optional garnish
- Salt, to taste

1 In a gallon stock pot, place the onions, garlic and sesame oil, and stir to coat. Cook and stir over medium-low heat until onions are completely caramelized and golden brown, about 20 minutes. Add the leeks, cover and turn heat to very low. Meanwhile, bring water to a boil in a large stock pot, with lemon grass, anise pods, ginger, peppercorns, cinnamon stick and miso. Stir, reduce heat to medium-low and simmer 30 minutes. Strain the spiced water into the caramelized leek and onion mixture. Simmer 10 minutes and taste; add more miso, salt and pepper if desired.

2 Add the rice noodles and carrots to onion pho and simmer 4-5 minutes, until noodles are tender. Divide among serving bowls. Garnish each bowl with Thai basil, chopped scallions, bean sprouts, minced chilis or a sprinkle of cayenne, lime wedges, and chopped cilantro and mint leaves, as desired.

MAKES 6 SERVINGS, ABOUT 2½ QUARTS

Pairing: A hoppy pale ale, such as Contessa from Birra Amiata, sparkles with the lemon grass and spices.

GRILLED TOMATO SOUP

Faced with a bushel of almost over-ripe tomatoes, I knew I had to use them up quickly. Yet it was too hot to can a batch of tomato sauce. A BBQ grill can cook all the tomatoes at once, away from the kitchen, and makes it super easy to slide off the papery tomato skins. Use a Vitamix or high speed blender to produce a creamy emulsion, or a stick blender to make a puree.

1 head garlic

4 pounds ripe tomatoes

3 tablespoons olive oil or olive oil cooking spray

Juice of one half lemon (about 2 tablespoons)

1 teaspoon fresh chopped thyme or ¼ teaspoon dried thyme

Salt

Pepper

6 tablespoons sour cream or cashew cream, page 156

Fresh chopped rosemary leaves, optional

Pairing: A malty Oktoberfest will match the roasty notes of the cooked garlic and tomatoes, or garnish with additional chopped fresh rosemary as a bridge, and pair with an IPA.

1 Preheat grill to 350°F. Wrap garlic in foil and place on hot grill. Rinse and slice tomatoes in half and brush or mist with olive oil. Place tomatoes cut side down on a clean grill mesh. Place the mesh on the hot grill, cover and cook 5 minutes. Remove grill mesh and set aside over a large baking sheet to collect juices. When cool enough to handle, peel away tomato skins and remove seeds. Place cooked tomato pulp in a blender with lemon juice. Cover and hold a tea towel over the blender lid. Blend on HIGH until smooth and creamy.

2 Remove garlic head from grill after it has cooked for 20 minutes. Let cool. Slide roasted garlic cloves out of the skins and add 2 tablespoons roasted garlic to the blender, along with fresh thyme and roasted tomato juices collected on the baking sheet. Blend on HIGH, mix well with pureed tomatoes, taste and add salt and pepper as desired. Garnish with sour cream or cashew cream.

MAKES 6 SERVINGS

MARKET VEGETABLE SOUP

By early September, our farmer's markets are overflowing with vegetables—zucchini, corn, celery, tomatoes, greens, broccoli and more. This soup uses whatever you have on hand, and tastes wonderful with the Pilsner Corn Bread, *page 177.*

- 1 tablespoon minced garlic
- 1 cup sliced onion
- 1 tablespoon olive oil
- 6 cups vegetable broth
- 1 cup chopped green beans
- 1 cup diced new potatoes
- 1 cup chopped carrots
- 1 cup chopped zucchini
- 1 cup chopped red bell pepper
- 1 cup chickpeas
- 1 cup chopped tomatoes
- ½ cup chopped celery
- 1 cup chopped broccoli florets
- ½ teaspoon dried rosemary
- ½ teaspoon dried thyme
- Salt and pepper, to taste
- 2 tablespoons chopped celery leaves

1 Place garlic, onion and oil in a large stock pot and sauté 5 minutes over low heat. Add broth and hard vegetables: green beans, potatoes, carrots, zucchini, bell pepper, and chickpeas, and bring to a boil over medium heat. Reduce heat to medium-low, stir and simmer 10 minutes, then add all the remaining ingredients, except the celery leaves. Simmer 10 minutes, add salt and pepper to taste, and garnish with chopped celery leaves.

MAKES 6 SERVINGS

PHOTO: MICHAEL WESSEL

Pairing: A zesty IPA brewed with citrus, or brown ale to provide caramel sweetness to offset the mixed vegetables and herbs.

KUZU-GINGER WHITE TEA BLEND

There comes a time in the life of every beer lover when over-indulgence leads to feeling hungover. While not a cure, this soothing broth will help heal the irritated stomach and reduce acidity, as kuzu is one of the most alkaline foods available. The broth may be prepared ahead of time and served chilled on its own, or blended with a fruit juice such as apple or pear.

- **1 tablespoon minced ginger root**
- **4 cups water**
- **3 tablespoons white tea leaves**
- **2 ounces cold water**
- **4 tablespoons organic kuzu powder (such as Eden Foods)**
- **3 tablespoons honey**

Pairing: Any Hair of the Dog will do.... (just kidding)

1 Bring ginger and water to a boil in a large saucepan, and remove from heat. Add white tea leaves and steep 5 minutes. Dissolve the kuzu powder in cold water, stirring well to make a slurry and remove lumps.

2 Strain the tea infusion back into a saucepan, discarding the leaves and ginger root, and place over low heat. Bring to simmer and whisk in the kuzu slurry and honey. Cook until thickened. Pour into a large cup and sip—the blend will be thickened but liquid enough to drink.

MAKES 3-4 SERVINGS

ASIAN VEGETABLE SOUP WITH LEMONGRASS

PHOTO: MICHAEL WESSEL

ASIAN VEGETABLE SOUP WITH LEMONGRASS

- 1 tablespoon peanut oil
- 1 tablespoon minced garlic
- 2 teaspoons minced lemongrass bulb
- 1 tablespoon grated fresh ginger root
- ½ teaspoon ground coriander
- 1 teaspoon turmeric
- 1 teaspoon tamari sauce
- ¼ teaspoon red chili pepper flakes
- 1 quart water
- 1 can (14 ounce) light coconut milk
- ⅓ cup chopped water chestnuts
- 1 cup chopped zucchini
- 2 cups baby spinach or bok choy, cleaned and chopped (loosely packed)
- ½ cup minced red onion, optional

1 Place peanut oil in a large stock pot over medium-low heat. Add garlic, lemongrass, ginger, coriander and turmeric. Stir to coat and sauté 5 minutes.

2 Add tamari sauce, red pepper flakes and water, cover and bring to a simmer over medium high heat. Turn heat to low, and stir in light coconut milk, water chestnuts, zucchini and spinach or bok choy. Cook until tender. Garnish with minced red onion. Taste and adjust seasonings, adding more tamari or pepper as desired.

MAKES 4 SERVINGS

Pairing: Dry Asian lager or hoppy Pilsner to cool the heat of ginger and pepper flakes.

Biere de Garde Jelly

BY CHRISTINA WARD

Milwaukee County Master Food Preserver & food preservation teacher

A jelly made from beer accentuates the flavors in the beer while removing most of the alcohol. The subtle dried fruit and spice notes traditionally associated with bière de garde yield a jelly with complex aromatics and caramel-brown color. The recipe uses as little sugar as possible while retaining the beer flavor.

You can use your jelly on toast as you would any other jelly, but also try as a glaze for fruits, cheeses, pastries, or spooned over ripe cheese such as Comte.

Many American craft brewers are creating amazing variations on this French style of beer, so choose your favorite for this recipe.

BIÈRE DE GARDE JELLY

750 ml bière de garde (22 oz. bottle)
750 ml organic apple juice, unfiltered
3 tablespoons (45 ml) lemon juice
2 tablespoons (30 grams) finely grated orange zest
⅔ cups (90 grams) low-sugar pectin
4 cups (404 grams) cane sugar

1. Decant beer into a heavy-bottom, non-reactive pot.
2. Add apple juice to bring total liquid to 1500 ml. Add lemon juice and orange zest.
3. Heat to boil, then reduce to simmer. Add sugar, stirring well to dissolve evenly.
4. Bring to full boil, add powdered pectin.[1] Stir until thoroughly mixed. Bring back to full, rolling boil. Boil for one minute.
5. Remove from heat and let rest about three minutes as you check for set.[2] Skim the jelly to remove foam scum.[3] Once set, begin processing.

PROCESSING

1. Clean and prep jars by washing with very hot soapy water, rinse thoroughly in hot water (do not dry them) immediately before use OR, run jars in a dishwasher on sanitize cycle before starting your jelly.
2. Place lids into boiling hot water. This sterilizes and softens the rubber edge on the lid to make a clean seal.
3. Pour jelly into hot, drained jars. Leave ¼ inch headspace. "Headspace" is the air left between the jelly and the rim of the jar, necessary to set seal.
4. Carefully wipe rims of jars to remove drips. Place lids on jars.
5. Place bands on jars and "finger tighten" (as soon as you feel the natural resistance of the band on the jar when turning, stop).
6. Place jars into boiling water processor. Jars should be on rack and not touching the bottom of the canning pot.
7. Process 10 minutes (timing begins when the water in the canner is at a full boil).
8. Remove jars from canner. Place jars on flat counter/table surface and let them cool 24 hours. Jars can take a full 24 hours to set up completely.

continued

BIÈRE DE GARDE JELLY CONTINUED

RECIPE FOOTNOTES

1 Pectin: powdered pectin is available at most grocery stores, but use a low-sugar brand such as Sure-jel or Pomona. At 49 grams per box, this recipe would take two boxes.

2 This is common to the jelly making process. The air and boiling will cause foam to rise to the top. Let the foam form a scum layer and as it cools, it will solidify. Use a small sieve, mesh skimmer or slotted spoon to remove the scum layer.

3 Checking the set: take about two teaspoons of the hot jelly out of the pot and place in a small dish. As it cools, it should thicken. After 3 minutes, use the "Moses" test: run your finger through the middle of the jelly in the dish, making a divide. If the jelly stays parted, you're good! If it runs back together, a rescue is required. Add one tablespoon lemon juice, plus pre-mixed ¼ cup cane sugar blended with ⅓ cup low-sugar pectin to the pot of jelly. Stir until thoroughly mixed. Bring back to boil over medium-high heat for one minute. Test again to ensure set.

4 The bands on the jars will be very loose...they should be! The bands serve as lid holders during processing and shock absorbers during travel. Your biere de garde jelly will be shelf stable for one year from the date you make it. Of course, once you open the jar, it should be refrigerated.

CHAPTER 12

FRUITS & DESSERTS

GRILLED PEACHES WITH HONEY-THYME GLAZE

PHOTO: JENNIFER MARX

GRILLED PEACHES WITH HONEY-THYME GLAZE

Grilled peaches with honey-thyme glaze match amazingly well with a simple salad of sliced endive and crumbled Gorgonzola. Prepare extra grilled peaches, and serve with French toast the next morning, or diced and mixed with yogurt or ice cream for dessert.

- **6 ripe white peaches**
- **2 tablespoons almond oil or walnut oil**
- **½ cup honey**
- **½ teaspoon fresh thyme leaves plus 4 sprigs thyme for garnish**

1 Prepare a grill for several minutes of cooking at medium heat, about 325° F. Wash and cut peaches in half. Remove the pits. Brush lightly with almond or walnut oil and place sliced side down on grill over direct heat. Allow fruit to sear with grill marks, about 30 seconds, then move to perimeter of grill to cook until soft, about 1 to 2 minutes more, depending on ripeness.

2 Muddle honey with ½ teaspoon fresh thyme leaves and the remaining oil and pour over grilled peaches on a platter. Garnish with remaining fresh thyme sprigs.

MAKES 6 SERVINGS (2 HALVES PER PERSON)

Pairing: A sprightly, unfiltered wheat ale makes a excellent foil to the sweet honey glaze, or a tart Belgian style ale brewed with herbs or flowers, such as hibiscus or calendula, would meld with the caramelized peach.

BROWN ALE BANANAS

PHOTO: JENNIFER MARX

BROWN ALE BANANAS

I think of this recipe as a summer staple—grilled bananas wrapped in a buckwheat crepe for brunch, grilled bananas and avocado salsa for veggie tacos, or grilled bananas, chopped hazelnuts and caramelized onion over rice for supper. You can also make this recipe with grilled plantains, as shown.

2 tablespoons butter
1 cup brown ale
1/8 teaspoon salt
4 ripe bananas
Pinch maple sugar or ½ teaspoon maple syrup

1 Melt butter in a large, cast iron skillet and whisk in brown ale and salt. Remove from heat. Peel bananas, slice in half lengthwise, and place in brown ale mixture. Prepare grill for several minutes of cooking over medium heat. Grill bananas on both sides over direct heat to obtain sear marks, and return to skillet placed on perimeter of grill grate. Cook until just tender and you can smell the bananas. Serve warm with ice cream for dessert, or other suggestions above.

MAKES 4 SERVINGS

Pairing: Highlight the nutty flavors of the brown ale with more of the same, such as a Rogue Hazelnut Brown or Lazy Magnolia Pecan Ale, or aim for a refreshing contrast with an Imperial Weizen or hoppy American riff on Belgian pale ale.

WATERMELON WITH BASIL & LIME

PHOTOÚ MICHAEL WESSEL

WATERMELON WITH BASIL & LIME

1 Whisk together lime juice, lime zest, basil chiffonade, salt, pepper and almond oil. Prepare onion and watermelon and toss with dressing in large serving bowl. Garnish with crumbled cheese and sprigs of basil.

- ¼ cup lime juice
- 1 teaspoon lime zest
- 2 tablespoons basil chiffonade
- ½ teaspoon salt
- Pinch ground white pepper (less than ⅛ teaspoon)
- 2 tablespoons almond oil
- ½ cup sweet onion, peeled and thinly sliced
- ½ ripe red watermelon, seeded and cubed (about 4 cups)
- ½ cup crumbled Cotija or sheep's milk feta cheese
- 8 sprigs basil

Tip: How to make a chiffonade of fresh herbs—clean the leaves and remove from the stems. Stack the leaves evenly and roll up sideways into a log shape, starting at one edge of the stack. Use a small sharp knife to slice the rolled leaves crosswise to make tiny ribbons.

Pairing: A pale American lager, such as Full Sail Session Lager, is mild enough to let the sweetness of the watermelon shine through the pairing, with just enough malt to match the salty, creamy taste of the Cotija cheese.

SPRECHER BLACK BAVARIAN AND CHOCOLATE-BURNT CARAMEL CREAM SHORTCAKES

PHOTO: ROGER BROWN

CHOCOLATE BURNT CARAMEL CREAM SHORTCAKES

CHOCOLATE SHORTCAKES

- 1⅓ cups flour
- 1 cup cocoa
- 1 teaspoon salt
- 1 tablespoon baking powder
- 1 teaspoon baking soda
- ½ cup sugar, plus more for sprinkles
- 1 cup heavy cream, plus 2-3 tablespoons, as needed
- ¼ cup black lager, such as as Black Bavarian
- ¼ cup butter, melted

1 Preheat oven to 425°F. Sift together 1 cup flour, cocoa, salt, baking powder, baking soda and sugar in a large mixing bowl. Mix ale and cream in a 2-cup measure, and slowly pour into the flour mixture, stirring as you pour. Gather the dough together, and if it feels dry, add a bit more cream. Gently pat dough on a floured surface (using the remaining ⅓ cup flour), until about ½-inch thick. Cut with a 2½-in. biscuit cutter to get 10 biscuits. Brush with melted butter. Place on baking sheet about 2 inches apart and bake 14-15 minutes, or until browned. Remove from oven and sprinkle with sugar. Let cool 20 minutes before splitting and filling for shortcakes.

BURNT CARAMEL CREAM

- ½ cup sugar
- 2 tablespoons water
- Pinch salt
- 1 teaspoon pure vanilla extract
- 1½ cups heavy whipping cream, at room temperature

YIELDS 1½ CUPS.

BURNT CARAMEL CREAM

1 In a small saucepan over medium heat, combine sugar, water, and salt; let sit until well blended. Cook, without stirring, until mixture turns a golden brown. Immediately remove from heat and stir in vanilla extract.

2 Let sugar syrup cool for 5 minutes, then gradually stir in lukewarm heavy cream. Return to medium heat, whisking until mixture is smooth. Scrape mixture into a glass bowl and cover; chill until very cold (about 3 hours). To assemble, beat the caramel cream until soft peaks form. Cover and refrigerate until ready to use.

continued

CHOCOLATE BURNT CARAMEL CREAM SHORTCAKES CONTINUED

NECTARINES

- 2 cups sliced nectarines
- ½ cup superfine or powdered sugar (adjust according to taste of fruit)
- Juice of one lemon wedge

> *Pairing:* Sprecher Black Bavarian echoes the dark chocolate flavors of the shortcakes, while the burnt caramel cream makes the ripe nectarines pop on the palate.

NECTARINES

1. Wash and slice nectarines into bowl. Stir in sugar and juice from one lemon wedge.

2. To assemble, split shortcakes and place bottom halves in a glass baking dish. Spoon nectarines over each and 2-3 tablespoons whipped cream, and place biscuit halves on top.

MAKES 10 SHORTCAKES

PHOTO: ROGER BROWN

S'MORES WITH BEER MARSHMALLOWS

Chef Sean Paxton makes his beer marshmallows with a rich Belgian ale, but I think a barleywine or doppelbock works well too. Choose a dry day with litle humidity to make these beer marshmallows as the filling for adult S'mores, made with graham crackers and semi-sweet chocolate. Use organic powdered sugar for best taste and texture. You may adjust water to soften gelatin according to humidity and elevation. The texture of bloomed gelatin should be thick and smooth, not grainy.

1 Soften gelatin in 4 to 5 ounces water in the bowl of a stand mixer. While gelatin softens, prepare 9×13-inch glass pan by buttering inside and sprinkling with powdered sugar to cover base and sides; shake pan so sugar is evenly applied.

2 Combine ale or barley wine, cane sugar, salt and corn syrup in a large, deep pot over medium-high heat, and bring to soft-ball stage, 238° F on a candy thermometer. Mixture will foam and turn caramel colored.

3 Place bowl with bloomed gelatin into a stand electric mixer fitted with the whisk attachment. Turn mixer to MEDIUM-LOW and slowly pour in hot syrup, whisking into bloomed gelatin until it starts to fluff. Do not whip too fast or the hot syrup will splatter. Whip until white and fluffy, about 10 minutes, adding vanilla extract during last minute.

continued

3 envelopes plain powdered gelatin (3 tablespoons)
4 to 5 ounces cold water
Unsalted butter for pan
¼ cup sifted organic powdered sugar for pan
4 ounces decanted (no foam) barley wine or strong ale
2 cups pure cane sugar
¼ teaspoon salt
6 ounces corn syrup
½ teaspoon Madagascar Bourbon vanilla extract
2 cups organic powdered sugar sifted with 2 tablespoons cornstarch
Graham crackers and semi-sweet chocolate bars

MAKES ABOUT 50 MARSHMALLOWS

S'MORES WITH BEER MARSHMALLOWS CONTINUED

4 Scrape mixture into prepared pan and spread evenly. Sprinkle top with 2-3 tablespoons powdered sugar-starch mixture. When cooled and set (from 30 minutes to 3 hours depending on humidity), turn slab out onto a cookie sheet dusted with half of the powdered sugar mixture. Slice into cubes with sharp knife or scissors dipped in warm water between each slice. Roll cubes in remaining powdered sugar mixture to coat evenly. Air-dry until not sticky (varies by humidity). Keeps up to 10 days in sealed container.

5 To make s'mores, top a half graham cracker with bittersweet chocolate and 1 toasted beer marshmallow. Cover with a graham cracker, and press to soften the chocolate.

PHOTO: MARK ROBERTS

TOASTED POUND CAKE WITH BERRIES & PECANS

Make the pound cake a day ahead of time so it's easy to slice, toast and top with Mascarpone cheese (I like the Crave Brothers brand) thinned with a little cream and powdered sugar, fresh raspberries and chopped pecans.

1 cup (2 sticks) plus 1 tablespoon unsalted butter, softened
2¼ cups cake flour
¼ teaspoon baking powder
½ teaspoon salt
1 cup sugar
4 large eggs, at room temperature
1½ teaspoons pure Madagascar Bourbon vanilla extract
4 ounces Mascarpone cheese
2 tablespoons cream
2 tablespoons powdered sugar
½ cup toasted and chopped pecans
1½ cups fresh raspberries

1 Place rack in center of oven and preheat to 325°F. Grease a large loaf pan (9x5x3) with 1 tablespoon butter, dust the pan with 1 tablespoon cake flour; tap out excess. Whisk together the remaining flour, baking powder and salt ina small bowl.

2 In the bowl of a stand mixer fitted with the paddle attachment, beat the butter until soft at HIGH speed, then turn mixer to MEDIUM speed and slowly pour in sugar. Beat until fluffy, about 2-3 minutes. Stop mixer and scrape the bowl with a rubber spatula. Turn speed to LOW and beat in eggs, one at a time, stopping the mixer and scraping the bowl after each addition.

3 Add half the flour mixture and stir with a spatula until just blended, scrape bowl, and mix in remaining flour on LOW speed. Scrape the bowl and blend in vanilla extract, and mix on LOW speed another 30 seconds, or until batter is smooth.

4 Scrape batter into prepared loaf pan, pressing with spatula. Run a knife lengthwise through the batter; tap the pan several times on the counter to settle the batter and remove air bubbles. Place in oven and bake until golden brown, 60 to 65 minutes.

5 Before removing from oven rack, check with toothpick to make sure center is completely baked. Remove from oven and cool 10 to 15 minutes in the pan, and then turn over onto a wire rack to cool completely.

5 Mix Mascarpone with cream and powered sugar. Serve each slice with berries, nuts and cream.

BROWN SUGAR BISCUITS WITH MOCHA-CHIP ICE CREAM

PHOTO: MICHAEL WESS

BROWN SUGAR BISCUITS WITH MOCHA-CHIP ICE CREAM

Tender and sweet, these biscuits adapted from a recipe by James Beard make an ideal base for ice cream or whipped cream filling. The flavors meld well with a chocolate stout or a bourbon barrel-aged Baltic porter.

- **2 cups all-purpose flour**
- **1 teaspoon salt**
- **2 teaspoons baking powder**
- **⅓ cup light brown sugar, lightly packed**
- **4 tablespoons unsalted butter, cold**
- **1 cup heavy cream, plus 1 to 2 tablespoons, as needed**
- **½ teaspoon vanilla extract**

1 Place flour, salt, baking powder and brown sugar into a large mixing bowl and whisk together until sugar is blended into flour without lumps. Cut the cold butter into small cubes, then mix into the flour mixture with a pastry cutter or two knives, until the mixture looks like corn meal.

2 Preheat oven to 400°F. Mix cream and vanilla extract in a measuring cup. Stir the flour mixture with one hand and slowly drizzle in the cream-vanilla blend, stirring until flour begins to bind. Add more cream if needed to make dough. With clean hands, scrape and press the dough into a ball and place on a lightly floured board or piece of parchment paper. Gently pat and fold the dough twice, and then pat into a rectangle about ⅔-inch thick.

3 Cut the dough into ten rounds about 2½ inches in diameter, gathering and gently re-forming dough scraps to make all the pieces, and place on a parchment-lined or nonstick baking sheet. Place in middle rack of oven and bake 12 to 15 minutes, or until puffed and golden-brown on top. Remove from oven and turn over so the bottoms of the biscuits don't over-brown. Let biscuits cool completely before splitting in half and filling with your favorite brand of ice cream, or the mocha-chip ice cream recipe below.

MAKES 10 SERVINGS

Pairing: Try a chocolate stout with bright carbonation, such as Bison Brewing Organic Chocolate Stout, to lighten the impact of the rich ice cream.

BROWN SUGAR BISCUITS WITH MOCHA-CHIP ICE CREAM CONTINUED

MOCHA CHIP ICE CREAM

- 5 ounces (fl) evaporated milk
- 2 cups heavy cream
- 1 egg yolk
- 1 teaspoon vanilla extract
- 2 tablespoons espresso powder
- 2 tablespoons ground bittersweet chocolate
- ¾ cup sugar plus more for garnish
- ½ cup chocolate chips (or more, to taste)

4 Mix evaporated milk, cream, egg yolk, vanilla extract, espresso powder, ground chocolate and sugar in a large saucepan, whisking until blended. Heat over medium low heat, mixing well with a long-handled whisk, until thickened and sugar is melted. Remove from heat and let cool. Freeze in an ice cream maker according to manufacturer's instructions, and add chocolate chips halfway through. Scrape ice cream into a re-sealable container and ripen the ice cream for 5 hours or more in the freezer.

MAKES 1 QUART ICE CREAM

Tip: Use a fine grater to grind a 1 ounce chunk of chocolate, or purchase a premade ground chocolate; however, do not substitute a powdered cocoa or hot chocolate drink mix.

PAPAYA & AVOCADO

Use a papaya that is very ripe: the skin will look mottled and ugly, but the fruit inside will be perfectly ripe. If you really love the taste of papaya, save a quarter-cup of the seeds to add to the citrus vinaigrette. They add a peppery note and slightly crunchy texture.

- **½ cup freshly squeezed orange juice**
- **¼ cup toasted sesame oil**
- **½ teaspoon grated lemon zest**
- **¼ teaspoon freshly ground black pepper**
- **1 tablespoon minced cilantro**
- **12 ounces papaya**
- **2 ounces red onion, thinly sliced (about ⅓ cup)**
- **½ cup yellow grape tomatoes or cherry tomatoes**
- **1 large ripe avocado (8 to 10 ounces)**
- **½ cup chopped celery leaves**

Pairing: Pair with a bright, zesty IPA brewed with fruity hops, such as Citra or Bavarian Mandarina.

1 To make dressing, blend orange juice, sesame oil, lemon zest, pepper and cilantro until smooth, either in a blender or whisked by hand in a small bowl.

2 Peel, halve, seed and dice the papaya into bite-sized cubes and place in a medium mixing bowl. Add the red onion. Wash and cut the grape or cherry tomatoes in half, and add to salad. Cut the avocado in half, remove pit, and slice. Arrange slices in a fan shape over the top of the salad. Sprinkle with chopped celery leaves. Pour dressing over salad, and serve.

MAKES 4 SERVINGS

RED PLUM GALETTE WITH CARAMEL MALT SAUCE

PHOTO: MICHAEL WESS

RED PLUM GALETTE WITH CARAMEL MALT SAUCE

A galette is a hand-formed pastry, baked with edges crimped just enough to hold a topping of sliced fruit. To make it even easier, I used the DuFour puff pastry to assemble this red plum galette in about a half-hour. Make the caramel malt sauce in advance.

1 Place oven rack in top third of oven, and preheat oven to 400°F. Roll out puff pastry to ¼-inch thickness on a lightly floured surface. Cut into 4x6 rectangles, or just wider than the largest plum's diameter. Slightly crimp edges and prick with the tines of a fork spaced about 1-inch apart. Sprinkle with sugar. Arrange on a parchment lined baking sheet, and bake until puffed and golden brown, about 15-20 minutes. Top with caramel malt sauce and slices of ripe red plums. Serve immediately.

2 In a 2-quart heavy saucepan, mix sugar, malt syrup and water until blended. Cook over medium-high heat until syrup is bubbling. Stop stirring and reduce heat to medium, and cook until deep caramel-amber in color.

3 Remove from heat, and using a long-handled wooden spoon to stir, carefully pour hot cream into the caramel syrup. It will splatter if you pour it all in at once, so pour in a thin, gentle stream, stirring with the pot tilted slightly away from you to avoid steam.

4 Stir until smooth, and if mixture seems lumpy, place the pot over low heat and cook and stir until smooth and creamy. Add the butter and vanilla extract, and stir until smooth.

MAKES 4-6 SERVINGS

1 sheet frozen puff pastry (about 1 pound), thawed
1 tablespoon flour
2 tablespoons sugar
Caramel malt sauce (recipe below)
3 large very ripe red plums (about 10 ounces wt)
1 cup sugar
2 tablespoons barley malt syrup or unhopped malt extract (Eden Foods makes a plain barley malt syrup)
¼ cup water
½ cup heavy cream, heated until hot
¼ cup salted butter
1 teaspoon vanilla extract

Pairing: A barleywine or stock ale offers a plummy, toffee flavor and gentle carbonation to match the buttery pastry and caramel sauce.

SWEET POTATO PUDDING WITH GINGER & APRICOTS

- **1½ pounds sweet potatoes (2 large)**
- **1 can unsweetened coconut milk (13.5 - 14 ounces fl)**
- **3 large eggs, separated**
- **½ cup dark brown sugar, packed**
- **½ cup flour**
- **pinch salt**
- **1 tablespoon cinnamon**
- **½ teaspoon fresh grated nutmeg**
- **2 tablespoons butter**
- **8 fresh apricots (about 10-12 ounces, total weight)**
- **1 tablespoon peeled and grated fresh ginger root**
- **¼ cup dark rum**
- **Garnish: whipped cream**

Pairing: For refreshing contrast, choose an apricot wheat ale or in winter, a warming rum barrel-aged strong ale works well.

1 Preheat oven to 400°F. Place sweet potatoes on a baking sheet lined with foil or parchment paper and pierce the potatoes several times with a fork or tip of a sharp knife to make steam vents. Bake until potatoes are soft and gooey —the juices will be bubbling out of the steam vents. Remove from oven and reduce heat to 350°F.

2 When cool, scrape the centers of the roasted sweet potatoes into a large mixing bowl. Discard the skins. Mash potatoes until smooth, then mash in coconut milk, egg yolks, brown sugar, flour, salt, cinnamon and nutmeg. Whip the egg whites in a quart mixing bowl until soft peaks form. Use a spatula to fold egg whites into the sweet potato batter. Scrape and spread the mixture into a lightly buttered 9x13x2-inch baking dish. Place in oven and bake 25 minutes.

3 While pudding bakes, place 1 tablespoon butter in a saucepan. Wash, pit and chop the apricots. Add the apricots to the saucepan and place over medium heat. Stir in ginger root and rum and bring to a simmer. When apricots soften, mix in rum, and remove from heat. Open the oven, and pull out rack with the baking dish; spoon the apricot mixture over the top of the sweet potato pudding and return to oven to bake 20-25 minutes more, or until golden brown. Remove from oven and let cool to lukewarm. Slice and serve with whipped cream, if desired.

MAKES 6-8 SERVINGS

BLACK CHERRY CRUMBLE

Cherries are a staple in Wisconsin, and I serve them with a simple, spicy oatmeal topping that makes this dessert possible to enjoy in less than an hour. For the garnish, I use the chocolate wafer disks made by TCHO, a San Francisco chocolatier that is a great supporter of the craft brewing community.

1 Preheat oven to 375°F. Place cherries in the bottom of an oven-safe 8-inch baking disk or pie pan. In a medium bowl, mix flour, brown sugar, oatmeal, butter, cinnamon and vanilla extract, until mixture forms pea-sized clumps. Sprinkle evenly over cherries and bake 25-30 minutes or until cherries are bubbly and topping is lightly browned. Serve with whipped cream and chocolate wafers or chips.

MAKES 4 TO 6 SERVINGS

- **2 cups frozen black cherries**
- **¼ cup all-purpose flour**
- **½ cup dark brown sugar**
- **½ cup rolled oats**
- **4 tablespoons unsalted butter, softened**
- **½ teaspoon cinnamon**
- **¼ teaspoon vanilla extract**
- **Garnish: whipped cream, chocolate wafers or chocolate chips**

Pairing: Cherry stout or black IPA

PHOTO: MICHAEL WESSEL

BLUEBERRY RICOTTA BEIGNETS WITH STOUT CHOCOLATE SAUCE

PHOTO: MICHAEL WESSEL

BLUEBERRY RICOTTA BEIGNETS WITH STOUT CHOCOLATE SAUCE

I like presenting these with a robust American amber ale or malty dark lager, to pick up the sweetness of the stout and chocolate, without overwhelming the blueberry and ricotta flavors.

- 2 large eggs
- ⅓ cup sugar
- 1 cup whole-milk ricotta
- 1 teaspoon vanilla extract
- ⅛ teaspoon salt
- 1 tablespoon baking powder
- ¾ cup flour
- Grapeseed oil
- ½ cup blueberries
- Stout chocolate sauce, recipe follows

1 Whisk together eggs, sugar, ricotta, vanilla, salt, baking powder and flour until smooth. Cover and refrigerate 2 hours, to let batter rest.

2 Place a 2-quart heavy saucepan on the stove and add grapeseed oil to a depth of 2½ inches. Turn heat to medium-high and bring to 350°F, testing temperature with a thermometer.

3 To make the beignets, mix blueberries into the batter and drop by the tablespoonful into the hot oil and fry, turning once with tongs or a mesh spoon, to cook until browned well on both sides. Cook 4-6 beignets at one time, so the pan doesn't get too crowded. Stir batter before making new batch, so every beignet has several blueberries (otherwise, they will sink to the bottom of the batter). Cook about 2 minutes on each side. Replenish oil to a depth of 2½ inches and allow oil to reheat to 350°F between batches.

4 Remove beignets and drain on paper towel or brown paper. Keep warm in oven or toaster oven until ready to serve. Serve warm with stout chocolate sauce.

MAKES 12-14 BIEGNETS

BLUEBERRY RICOTTA BEIGNETS WITH STOUT CHOCOLATE SAUCE CONTINUED

This recipe is adapted from one by Rose Ann Finkel, using the Pike's XXXXX—Chocolate Sauce. She cautions, "Do not use chocolate chips as they are too waxy!" This recipe also appeared in my cookbook, THE BEST OF AMERICAN BEER AND FOOD (Brewers Publications, 2007).

STOUT CHOCOLATE SAUCE

- 8 bittersweet chocolate (at least 60 percent cocoa) finely chopped
- 1 cup heavy cream
- 4 ounces (fl) Pike XXXXX Stout (you could substitute an available dry stout or milk stout, if you like it sweeter)
- 1 teaspoon vanilla extract (preferably Madagascar Bourbon Vanilla)

5 Place the chopped chocolate in a quart mixing bowl. Mix cream and stout in a saucepan and bring to a simmer over medium-high heat. Remove from heat, and pour over the chopped chocolate. Gently whisk until the chocolate melts and sauce is smooth. Whisk in the vanilla and serve warm, or cool completely and store in an airtight container in the refrigerator. May be held for up to one week.

MAKES 2 CUPS

STRAWBERRY & WITBIER GELEE

When strawberries are ripe and in season, that's the time to make this berry beer gelee. Think Midwestern jello salad, but presented with far more panache.

12 **ounces witbier**
1 **pound very ripe strawberries, cleaned, divided**
¼ **cup plus 2 tablespoons superfine or caster sugar**
2 **tablespoons unflavored gelatin**
1 **cup water**
1 **cup heavy cream**
2 **tablespoons orange liqueur or strawberry liqueur (Italian Fragole)**

1 Pour the witbier into the center of a 2-quart glass measuring cup. Allow foam and carbonation to settle. Save 6 berries for garnish; trim and finely dice the remaining strawberries. Mix witbier, diced berries and juices and ¼ cup sugar. Cover and let rest for 1 hour.

2 Stir the witbier-berry mixture. Sprinkle the unflavored gelatin over 1 cup cold water in a medium saucepan. Stir with a spoon and dissolve (bloom) for 5 minutes until softened, then place over medium heat and bring to a simmer.

3 When gelatin blend simmers, remove from heat and whisk into the beer-berry mixture; the mixture will foam a bit. Pour into a 9x13x2-inch dish. Let cool to lukewarm, then cover and chill until solid.

4 Remove the pan from the refrigerator, and slice gelee into 1–inch cubes. Return to refrigerator to keep cold. Whip the heavy cream, liqueur and 2 tablespoons sugar, until soft peaks form. Divide the witbier gelee between 6 dessert dishes. Top each with 2 tablespoons whipped cream and sliced strawberry garnish.

MAKES 6 SERVINGS

Pairing: A chocolate bock beer or chocolate stout makes an ideal complement to strawberries and cream in this delicate dish. A chocolate cherry stout such as New Glarus Brewing Co. or Bell's Beer tastes rich

Note: Beer blogger Derrick Peterman experimented with raspberry lambic jello (August 2009, The Session), and found that by heating the lambic, the flavor of the beer turned earthy. My take: most traditional lambics are brewed with aged hops that turn funky when heated. Adding fresh fruit increases the acidity and retains fruit flavor.

RECIPE INDEX

RECIPE INDEX

INGREDIENT INDEX

INGREDIENT INDEX

INGREDIENT INDEX

INGREDIENT INDEX

INGREDIENT INDEX

INGREDIENT INDEX

INGREDIENT INDEX

INGREDIENT INDEX

INGREDIENT INDEX

PHOTO INDEX, PARTICIPATING BREWERIES

ABOUT THE AUTHOR: Lucy Saunders thinks of beer as food and has championed the presence of craft beer at the American table for over 20 years. She conducts tastings at cooking schools, retailers, and nonprofit groups, including the Smithsonian, American Cheese Society, American Homebrewers Association and the Craft Brewers Conference. She has worked with the Association of Food Journalists, the International Association of Culinary Professionals, the American Culinary Federation and other groups. Saunders is the author of COOKING WITH BEER (1996), GRILLING WITH BEER (2006), and THE BEST OF AMERICAN BEER & FOOD (2007). She lives in Milwaukee, WI.